2022

A Book of
Grace-Filled
Days

LORETTA PEHANICH

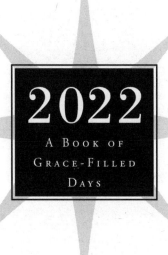

2022

A BOOK OF
GRACE-FILLED
DAYS

LOYOLAPRESS.
A JESUIT MINISTRY
Chicago

LOYOLA PRESS.
A JESUIT MINISTRY

www.loyolapress.com

Cover and interior design by Kathy Kikkert.

ISBN: 978-0-8294-5041-5
Library of Congress Control Number: 2021936420

Printed in the United States of America.
21 22 23 24 25 26 27 28 29 30 Lake Book 10 9 8 7 6 5 4 3 2 1

INTRODUCTION

Life is better when you look for grace every day. Scripture yields riches when explored prayerfully, and you just might discover a gold mine of grace.

Ordinary things also lead to valuable discoveries. For example, one day while I sat quietly, my eyes were drawn to a single shiny whirligig spinning wildly on the patio. I watched as it cast bright beams on the family-room floor. Light multiplied, and I sensed God saying, "See? One small movement makes a whirlwind of difference. Never underestimate goodness and what you will do today, even if it feels like you're just spinning your wheels."

I never expected such reflections when I sat down that morning. Grace found me. It didn't require much, just as it took only a small breeze to spin that yard ornament. I was simply making a few minutes for prayer in a busy life. And

God who is in all things revealed a truth: God is waiting to be noticed.

God loves when people pay attention to the glimmers of grace waiting to be uncovered and used. A book like this offers you a way to plan and devote time to your relationship with God. And this book based on lectionary passages connects you to every person who is celebrating the liturgy every day, whether you and I are participating in Mass or not. We pray together as a team. You are there for me, and I'm here for you. A world community of believers is praying, praising, growing, serving, and connecting as a result.

When all our simple breaths come together, in seemingly small prayers, we become a force like a strong, driving wind. It's really God's doing; we just need to show up daily for prayer.

Even when people forget to pray or avoid it, God is constantly on the lookout, hoping to be noticed. Sometimes, grace looks for you. God longs for you and me and wants this time of reflection even more than we do. So, don't give up! Remember that St. Luke, whose Gospel we hear on Sundays this year, is interceding and praying alongside us. We are invited to ask for what we need. The divine One can't wait to shower graces upon us but wants to be asked. I've been asking regularly as I wrote that you be blessed by this book, and I expect goodness to flourish in all of us as a result. Allow God's presents.

God communicates uniquely with each human being. One person senses God in dreams, like Joseph. Another hears God best in music. A third meets God through sensations in the body. But everybody has an imagination. Picture a plate of warm brownies straight out of the oven. You've just used your imagination, and I bet if you compared your plate with others, various images would surface. Some brownies would be huge, some frosted, some marbled or blonde, and others would contain walnuts (not mine!) or be sugar free. God can and frequently does communicate in images. You might be tempted to discount ideas that "just come to you," but God-given insights are real. This book contains some invitations to imagine yourself in a scene with Jesus, having a conversation with Christ, and encouraging a sense of surprise, which is often a sign of God at work. This kind of prayer might lead you to annotate your key thoughts.

Many of us were taught never to write in books, which are treasures to be cared for and respected. Some think it's almost sinful to bend the corner of a page, and no one considers it ethical to deface library-book pages with drawings or comments.

The book you now hold is quite different. Write in it! Fold a page! Mark a favorite passage. Draw symbols in it. Unless people in a household are sharing it, you get to personalize it. Or maybe more than one person *can* write in the margins. Underline a word that speaks to you. Add an exclamation point if you want. Write a rebuttal at the bottom of a page. You are invited to treat this book like a journal. Talk to God through your pen. Imagine how Jesus would respond to your questions. Maybe you will want to write at the top of the page the word that struck you most. God might speak to you between the lines. Rereading what you've written monthly might help you better notice in retrospect where God has been whispering. Imagine how easy a year-end *examen* could be if you did this. It might reveal a pattern over several months that you otherwise may have missed. (An *examen* is an Ignatian prayer practice that involves seeking the Holy Spirit's light, giving thanks, and reviewing the day as God sees it. Not meant to be a listing of sins, the *examen* may lead the soul to ask forgiveness. It ends with a focus on tomorrow and how we intend to live.)

I have no idea what 2022 will hold. It's a mystery. But I trust that our wondrous God will use the words on these pages to communicate personally with you. One sentence may cause you to think of a completely different idea. Your mind might wander to a connected and more personally relevant topic. God's gusts of love are going to waft through your soul. Today is going to be a grace-filled day. Watch for it.

NOVEMBER 28

• FIRST SUNDAY OF ADVENT •

The days are coming, says the LORD,
when I will fulfill the promise
I made.
—JEREMIAH 33:14

Happy new liturgical year! It's countercultural to begin a new year in November while society prepares for the old year ending. A new year offers a fresh start. Christ's return is closer than it was yesterday, and who knows if he will arrive tomorrow. Christ's arrival at the end of days is a reason for joy and hope. Meanwhile, people plan holiday travel, year-end donations, and gifts. Preparations long underway will soon be complete. Christians believe that God will fulfill the promise of heaven. What more needs to be done to prepare for *that* meeting? Attachments to this life hamper a free anticipation of heaven. The beginning of Advent is the perfect time to ask God for the grace to be spiritually free.

Jeremiah 33:14–16
Psalm 25:4–5,8–9,10,14 (1b)
1 Thessalonians 3:12—4:2
Luke 21:25–28,34–36

NOVEMBER 29

In days to come,
The mountain of the LORD's house
shall be established as the highest mountain.
—ISAIAH 2:2

Flying into Seattle, I always gasp at the breathtaking view of Mount Rainier. Even when rain clouds obscure its base, the high snowy peak protrudes above the clouds. The native peoples called it Tahoma, which in one translation means "the mother of waters." Some say they believed it to be God's body protruding from earth. Such a marvel of creation reminds me that God is almighty and capable of breathtaking possibilities. I watch for the mountain whenever I fly. And I long for a glimpse of Mount Rainier as a sign that I am arriving at my destination. God, who is high above all, is my destination too, even when it's "raining." God is present even when obscured by clouds of trials.

Isaiah 2:1–5
Psalm 122:1–2,3–4b,4cd–5,6–7,8–9
Matthew 8:5–11

Tuesday

NOVEMBER 30

• ST. ANDREW, APOSTLE •

As Jesus was walking by the Sea of Galilee,
he saw two brothers.
—MATTHEW 4:18

In John's Gospel, Andrew followed John the Baptist, who
signaled to his disciples, "Behold the Lamb of God!" Perhaps
Andrew ran to the shore to tell his brother Peter. Can you
imagine his brother's reaction? "Get in the boat and get to
work," Peter may have chided his sibling. "Chasing another
local prophet? Tell me about this messiah as we fish." Perhaps
Andrew does just that, convincing Peter before Jesus walks
up in today's Gospel. The brothers hear Christ's call together
and drop everything immediately. Urgency drives them to
abandon the family business to their partners. Such
spontaneity! Or is it that Jesus called so distinctly that they
knew they needed to follow? What was it about these
brothers that caused Jesus to single them out to be his close
friends?

Romans 10:9–18
Psalm 19:8,9,10,11
Matthew 4:18–22

Wednesday
DECEMBER 1

The LORD is my shepherd; I shall not want.
—PSALM 23:1

This well-known psalm reminds us that we lack nothing. We have plenty, even when we fear that we're deprived. We have enough time, enough patience, enough stamina, enough love, and enough graces because God is our leader and protector. Even when we fear we will run out, we have access to all that we need. Abundance is part of being Christian. That's what makes it easier to give away our time, treasure, and talents. We have faith that the Shepherd will take care of every need; even if we get lost, the Shepherd will come looking for us and restore us. We lack nothing that is necessary to living a full life.

Isaiah 25:6–10a
Psalm 23:1–3a,3b–4,5,6
Matthew 15:29–37

DECEMBER 2

On that day they will sing this song in the land of Judah.
—ISAIAH 26:1

On this day, you can sing even if you don't like your voice.
Your pen can hum as you scribble, doodle, and add musical
notes in the margins of this book or your journal. Just as
Isaiah's readers celebrated and praised God's
accomplishments, you can draw an asterisk, underline, or
highlight as a way of praying. Maybe a phrase warrants
colored pens to augment your reflections. Today Isaiah
mentions a strong city. Maybe you will outline a skyline as
you meditate on that. Later, you may look back during an
end-of-month prayer review and remember why this or a
different page stood out for you. Let writing implements
participate in prayer. In days to come, you can flip to noted
pages when you want to repeat or deepen a prayer. Let
yourself create.

Isaiah 26:1–6
Psalm 118:1 and 8–9,19–21,25–27a
Matthew 7:21,24–27

Jesus appeared to the Eleven and said to them:
"Go into the whole world
and proclaim the Gospel to every creature."
—MARK 16:15

Imagine being St. Ignatius's college buddy, as St. Francis was. Where might you go to study together? What would you like to discuss? Both came from families associated with royalty. St. Francis and St. Ignatius influenced each other's thinking; they shared a zeal to preach abroad. Inspired by this friendship, today's saint was one of the first seven Jesuits to take vows in Paris. When they bade farewell to one another as St. Francis headed to evangelize in eastern Asia, it was the last time they saw each other. That must have been emotional. Proclaiming the Good News had a cost. Think about what zeal means to you, and where you express it.

MEMORIAL
1 Corinthians 9:16–19,22–23
Psalm 117:1bc,2
Mark 16:15–20

DECEMBER 4

• ST. JOHN DAMASCENE, PRIEST AND DOCTOR OF THE CHURCH •

Jesus went around to all the towns and villages.
—MATTHEW 9:35

Once Jesus left home, it seems he traveled constantly. But it was purposeful movement: teaching, proclaiming, and curing. St. John, born in Damascus, also traveled; he went to a monastery, where he wrote extensively to proclaim the Gospel while living under a Muslim government. Acts of teaching and proclaiming the Gospel often require leaving home, even if it's just to the local parish meeting room. In every corner of the world, people are spreading the Gospel. God's word is on the move. May our hearts be moved, as Christ's was, by the sight of others in need. What words of healing can we offer today to someone in need?

Isaiah 30:19–21,23–26
Psalm 147:1–2,3–4,5–6
Matthew 9:35—10:1,5a,6–8

Sunday

DECEMBER 5

• SECOND SUNDAY OF ADVENT •

I am confident of this,
that the one who began a good work in you
will continue to complete it
until the day of Christ Jesus.
—PHILIPPIANS 1:6

God started something wonderful by thinking of you and bringing you into being. God loves the person you are, knowing that you will participate through your free choices in the work of bringing God's love to others. And every time you show love, you become more of what God hopes you to be. You are part of a community that hopes for the day of Christ Jesus. Advent can be a time to patiently reconsider how you contribute to the goodness in creation. You can live in the reign of God now through participating in love. Invite God into this day and let God lead.

Baruch 5:1–9
Psalm 126:1–2,2–3,4–5,6 (3)
Philippians 1:4–6,8–11
Luke 3:1–6

Say to those whose hearts are frightened:
Be strong, fear not!
Here is your God
. . . he comes to save you.
—ISAIAH 35:4

And still I worry. Jesus says not to, and yet I do. God smiles and reaches out for me again. My Abba never wants me to falter out of fear that God doesn't love me. God always loves. God is always present. Flaws and brokenness don't diminish my value. I am loved just as I am. Still, I need a pep talk: Be strong! Fear nothing! God is here. I am encouraged to leave certain tendencies behind: negative self-talk, complaints, attitudes of entitlement, judgment, careless thinking, and food as a medicant. I can't pour from an empty cup, nor can I serve others when I'm trapped in fear.

Isaiah 35:1–10
Psalm 85:9ab and 10,11–12,13–14
Luke 5:17–26

DECEMBER 7

• ST. AMBROSE, BISHOP AND DOCTOR OF THE CHURCH •

*It is not the will of your
heavenly Father
that one of these little ones be lost.*
—MATTHEW 18:14

People feel adrift in many ways, such as discouragement over
a dead-end job, a broken relationship, or pending holidays
that, this year, will be celebrated for the first time without a
certain loved one. It's not God's desire that people feel lost.
The mortal enemy of humanity, however, loves to see people
sapped and sad. Each person is one of God's little ones, even
when we think we're running everything. It doesn't take
much to reach out to another human being who is feeling
down. It can help lift one's own doldrums by focusing on
someone else. Let God move you to help another person; in
so doing, you help yourself.

Isaiah 40:1–11
Psalm 96:1–2,3 and 10ac,11–12,13
Matthew 18:12–14

DECEMBER 8

Blessed be the God and Father of our Lord Jesus Christ,
who has blessed us in Christ
with every spiritual blessing.
—EPHESIANS 1:3

Catholics gather as a family at Mass today to talk with Jesus'
mom. What a tremendous blessing to have access to Mary in
prayer. We might tell her our deepest thoughts and ask for
miracles. Mary takes her vulnerable children to Jesus. When
Mary appeared to St. Catherine Laboure in 1830 and asked
that a medal of the Immaculate Conception be made,
miracles happened. Just as loving mothers often seem to pull
miracles out of hats, Mary knows exactly what to do. She
brings us to the great Miracle Worker, Jesus.

Genesis 3:9–15,20
Psalm 98:1,2–3ab,3cd–4
Ephesians 1:3–6,11–12
Luke 1:26–38

Thursday

DECEMBER 9

• ST. JUAN DIEGO CUAUHTLATOATZIN, HERMIT •

I will set in the wasteland the cypress,
together with the plane tree and the pine,
That all may see and know,
observe and understand,
That the hand of the LORD has done this.
—ISAIAH 41:19–20

In Mexico City, Our Lady of Guadalupe's shrine draws countless visitors to see the image of Mary known as *La Morenita* (The Little Black Madonna). It appears on a garment that delivered roses in December. God intervenes in history in unexpected ways using surprising means. Flowers signaled for Juan Diego and church authorities that God was at work, just as in today's passage something like a redwood miraculously grew in a desert. Through the Mother of God, our Lord helps in times of greatest need. Mary holds many titles; the church gives us three days in a row to ponder her roles.

Isaiah 41:13–20
Psalm 145:1 and 9,10–11,12–13ab
Matthew 11:11–15

Jesus said to the crowds:
"To what shall I compare this generation?
It is like children who sit in marketplaces."
—MATTHEW 11:16

In 2019, Pope Francis added the feast of Our Lady of Loreto to all calendars and liturgical books. Loreto, Italy, honors the house of Mary of Nazareth. You can contemplate visiting her home, where you always will find a welcome. No matter your situation, she leads to her Son. Perhaps you see yourself meeting her at a marketplace in town. She brings you to her front door and invites you in. Spend time at her kitchen table, where she pours you tea. After your comfortable conversation with Mary, Jesus enters the room to talk with you. You may wish to imagine yourself in Mary's guest bed, so sick from poor choices that you cannot move. Allow Mary to comfort you. Soon she will be calling her son in to heal you.

Isaiah 48:17–19
Psalm 1:1–2,3,4 and 6
Matthew 11:16–19

Saturday

DECEMBER 11

• ST. DAMASUS I, POPE •

*Take care of this vine,
and protect what your right hand has planted.*
—PSALM 80:15–16

Scripture is full of horticultural images. From the first couple in Eden to Mary Magdalene mistaking Jesus for a gardener after his resurrection, people have encountered holy moments in gardens, which demonstrate something profound about God. What comes to your mind when you picture a vineyard planted by God? God planted each of us in this place for some specific purpose. Jesus, the vine, provides to the branches a plentiful supply of nourishing grace that produces fruit the world really needs.

May we praise, reverence, and serve God wherever grace takes us. It may require an act of will to trust in the compassionate hand of God, whose watering can of grace and love gives life.

Sirach 48:1–4,9–11
Psalm 80:2ac and 3b,15–16,18–19
Matthew 17:9a,10–13

DECEMBER 12

• THIRD SUNDAY OF ADVENT •

"What should we do?"
—LUKE 3:10

So many people are looking for a leader or someone to tell them what to do. If only everything were simply all right or all wrong, with no vague areas. Deep within every person is a moral compass, set by God, to help us navigate a cloudy world. Life's storms come, and the ship is tossed. It's tempting to abdicate to someone providing easy answers. God provides graces and gifts to help us sort through enigmatic situations. Mentors and spiritual directors help but don't replace God, who lives within the human conscience, which the church teaches is primary. In a world full of fear—where we may be driven to decisions based on anxiety—let's turn prayerfully to God for the graces of discernment. May we choose what is most loving, kind, and worthy of our relationship with God.

Zephaniah 3:14–18a
Isaiah 12:2–3,4,5–6 (6)
Philippians 4:4–7
Luke 3:10–18

The utterance of one who hears what God says,
and knows what the Most High knows.
—NUMBERS 24:4

How do I know if I *hear* God within? Sometimes God provides a clear insight or an obvious path. At other times I need to use reason to help me hear God. It might take time. It helps if I'm in a state of balance (peace, equilibrium). I might think about how I'd advise a friend in my circumstances, which gives me a little distance when I'm too close to an issue. Or I can ask a prayerful friend for a second opinion. God would never lead me away from the commandments to love God and to love people. If I feel peace, joy, and an increase of faith or hope, it's likely God is guiding my decision.

Numbers 24:2–7,15–17a
Psalm 25:4–5ab,6 and 7bc,8–9
Matthew 21:23–27

DECEMBER 14

• ST. JOHN OF THE CROSS, PRIEST AND DOCTOR OF THE CHURCH •

Jesus said to the chief priests and the elders
of the people:
"What is your opinion?
A man had two sons."
—MATTHEW 21:28

Jesus is interested in your opinion! You can be honest with
Jesus and tell him exactly what you think. God knows you
learn and get to know yourself better by sharing your
thoughts with God. And if you need more prodding, look at
the numerous encouraging ideas in today's readings: Be
radiant with joy. You need not be ashamed of your deeds.
God hears you when you cry out. The Lord is close to the
brokenhearted. God will purify the people. Don't fret about
proud braggarts. Even Jesus' story of two sons is an
encouragement: your positive behaviors count more than
your hasty words.

Zephaniah 3:1–2,9–13
Psalm 34:2–3,6–7,17–18,19 and 23
Matthew 21:28–32

DECEMBER 15

*"Are you the one who is to come, or should we
look for another?"*
—LUKE 7:19

Some days are really rocky, and for whatever reason, we get
stuck or confused. Doubt creeps in, as it may have for John
the Baptist in today's passage. We may question whether,
with only ten days until Christmas, we'll be ready. We may
have stressful preparations yet to make. Distractions of the
perfect gift, the sensitive relative, or a lonely night can tilt
our focus away from Christ. We wonder if we are really
celebrating Jesus' birthday at all. God doesn't mind when we
bring up questions. "Will I be ready when you come, Jesus?"
Perhaps a prayer of faith-filled determination will help. Jesus,
we trust in you.

Isaiah 45:6c–8,18,21c–25
Psalm 85:9ab and 10,11–12,13–14
Luke 7:18b–23

DECEMBER 16

He who has become your husband is your Maker.
—ISAIAH 54:5

Women in religious communities talk about Jesus as their spouse. Some priests wear wedding rings to show the same spousal commitment to Jesus. Since Old Testament times, God has encouraged the people of Israel to think of God as a spouse. It's a very intimate relationship. Since I've been married for forty-three years, people will ask me, "What's your secret?" I often say it's forgiveness and a willingness to overlook things. Successful spouses expect goodness from each other and bring out the best in each other. God invites us into relationship with great tenderness to accept love beyond measure.

Isaiah 54:1–10
Psalm 30:2 and 4,5–6,11–12a and 13b
Luke 7:24–30

Obed became the father of Jesse, Jesse the father of David the king.
—MATTHEW 1:5B–6

My father's father was one of twelve children, seven of whom immigrated to the United States. Some of his siblings had nine and ten children. Every summer our family picnic drew more than one hundred people from just my grandfather's and his sister's branches. Three more generations have been born since then, and it's impossible for me to know all my relatives, both here and in "the old country." Some days I see someone who looks like Uncle Emil and wonder if we're first cousins twice removed. And then there are DNA tests that take us back centuries. How might I be related to the family of Obed? To you? Jesus' genealogy connects every one of us. Through Jesus' family tree and the Eucharist, we really are all relations.

Genesis 49:2,8–10
Psalm 72:1–2,3–4ab,7–8,17
Matthew 1:1–17

Blessed be the LORD, the God of Israel,
who alone does wondrous deeds.
And blessed forever be his glorious name;
may the whole earth be filled with his glory.
—PSALM 72:18–19

Maybe you've heard of the mnemonic for the four reasons for prayer: ACTS. It stands for adoration, contrition, thanks, and supplication. Which of the four is uppermost for you today: expressing praise, sorrow, needs, or gratitude? Adoration doesn't come as easily as asking for things, but the Creator loves to hear words of praise. As you look back on the past week, consider a "particular *examen*" during which you have adored God. A particular *examen* is a prayer in which you select a single quality such as patience or humility and review where that specific grace has been present. You may surprise yourself.

Jeremiah 23:5–8
Psalm 72:1–2,12–13,18–19
Matthew 1:18–25

Behold, I come to do your will.
—HEBREWS 10:7B

It is true that God speaks to each human heart and invites a response. But God speaks differently based on how people listen. Some get a mental picture or a feeling. For Mary, it was an honest-to-goodness angel, and for Elizabeth, it was a stirring in her womb. For some, an idea pops out of nowhere. God can use anything—from a chance remark to a song lyric—to communicate very personally with each person. And God does. It takes both faith and courage to press on to fulfillment when you hear a word "spoken" to you. What other graces are required to follow through and say an unrestrained yes! when God presents something to you?

Micah 5:1–4a
Psalm 80:2–3,15–16,18–19 (4)
Hebrews 10:5–10
Luke 1:39–45

Behold, you will conceive in your womb and bear a son,
and you shall name him Jesus.
He will be great and will be called Son of the
Most High.
—LUKE 1:31–32

In the *Spiritual Exercises* of St. Ignatius Loyola, retreatants imagine the mystery of the Incarnation. They take time to picture the Trinity looking over the entire surface of the earth, watching people making disastrous choices, hurting one another, and making a general mess of things. The Trinity begins nodding to one another: *It's time.* They commission a powerful angel to visit Mary, to ask her permission for the second Person of the Trinity to become a human being. They request a simple woman to birth the Savior of humanity, which is incapable of saving itself. God had this incredible plan all along. And it depended on a woman saying yes.

Isaiah 7:10–14
Psalm 24:1–2,3–4ab,5–6
Luke 1:26–38

Tuesday

DECEMBER 21

• ST. PETER CANISIUS, PRIEST AND DOCTOR OF THE CHURCH •

Our soul waits for the LORD,
who is our help and shield.
—PSALM 33:20

Our lives and world seem full of mayhem. Yet from Old
Testament times we hear that we have no need to fear any
upcoming trial. The speakers don't say that troubles will be
nonexistent; they say that we won't need to be afraid of them.
Somehow, God will give us the strength to withstand
difficulties. We are stronger than we know. And if the
problems become insurmountable, God will offer a way out,
teaches St. Paul, so that we'll be able to bear them. Rather than
fear God's punishments, embrace God's limitless forgiveness.
No troubles need destroy us. During dark days, it takes an act
of faith to be able to say, "God *is* with us." God is.

Song of Songs 2:8–14 or Zephaniah 3:14–18a
Psalm 33:2–3,11–12,20–21
Luke 1:39–45

DECEMBER 22

Mary said:
My soul proclaims the greatness of the Lord;
my spirit rejoices in God my savior.
—LUKE 1:46

It's not too late to ask Mary to help you as you consider Christ's birthday gift. She can assist you in discerning what her son really wants from you for his birthday. Your joy at the awareness of Christ among us is one welcome gift she might suggest. You could offer a burst of praise, as she did.

And Christ would enjoy the gift of you befriending the hungry, the sick, the imprisoned, and those without shelter. You still have time to pay attention for hints about the most important gift of all. Remember, the joy is in giving.

1 Samuel 1:24–28
1 Samuel 2:1,4–5,6–7,8abcd
Luke 1:46–56

Thursday

DECEMBER 23

• ST. JOHN OF KANTY, PRIEST •

Yes, he is coming, says the LORD of hosts.
But . . . who can stand when he appears?
—MALACHI 3:1B–2A

With Christmas two days away, I need to amend my
expectations of what I can get done. Goodbye to some
preparations for a major family gathering! I need to let go of
an idyllic photo of a kneeling Madonna and a baby in a
manger, too. Mary was probably exhausted, Joseph worried,
and traveling companions stressed. Like me right now. A
great consolation: traditions that don't fade. For example,
whenever I put up the Christmas tree, Handel's *Messiah*
accompanies the work. Melodic solos trill Scriptures like this
one from Malachi. God is like a "refiner's fire." Help me
refine my expectations, Lord, of what will make a great
celebration of your birth.

Malachi 3:1–4,23–24
Psalm 25:4–5ab,8–9,10 and 14
Luke 1:57–66

DECEMBER 24

The LORD also reveals to you
that he will establish a house for you.
—2 SAMUEL 7:11

Perhaps God was asking, "Who do you think you are? Ha ha!
You want to make *me* a house? That is just so funny. Do you
think you can control and contain me in a box? I made the
most incredible house already; it's the human heart. I've been
with you wherever you went. I've had my eye on you every
single moment of your life! You keep forgetting that. Think
about these promises: I will fix you a place, give you rest
from all enemies, and help you change thoughts that you
allow to hurt you. I'll be your loving father—your daddy. I'll
raise up an heir, my Son, and his kingdom will be eternal. If
you want to do something for me, then love. Just love!
Everything boils down to that."

2 Samuel 7:1–5,8b–12,14a,16
Psalm 89:2–3,4–5,27 and 29
Luke 1:67–79

When the angels went away from them to heaven,
the shepherds said to one another,
"Let us go, then, to Bethlehem
to see this thing that has taken place."

—LUKE 2:15

In the song "The Little Drummer Boy," a shepherd struggles with what gift to give Jesus. Jesus smiles when the boy offers his skills with a drum. What do I do that makes Jesus smile? Does God laugh when some of my habits surface, or when I make feeble attempts to control my life? Does God smile when I'm kind to someone without being asked or when I bite my tongue when tempted to say something mean? God, the giver, offers me an eternal smile as he holds out the gift of his only Son.

VIGIL:	DAWN:
Isaiah 62:1–5	Isaiah 62:11–12
Psalm 89:4–5,16–17,27,29 (2a)	Psalm 97:1,6,11–12
Acts 13:16–17,22–25	Titus 3:4–7
Matthew 1:1–25 or 1:18–25	Luke 2:15–20
NIGHT:	**DAY:**
Isaiah 9:1–6	Isaiah 52:7–10
Psalm 96:1–2,2–3,11–12,13	Psalm 98:1,2–3,3–4,5–6 (3c)
Titus 2:11–14	Hebrews 1:1–6
Luke 2:1–14	John 1:1–18

DECEMBER 26

• THE HOLY FAMILY OF JESUS, MARY, AND JOSEPH •

Thinking that he was in the caravan,
they journeyed for a day
and looked for him among their relatives
and acquaintances.
—LUKE 2:44

It's possible that Jesus had some relatives who made family get-togethers difficult, just like many families experience today. Perhaps his Uncle Uri drank too much and criticized without restraint. Maybe a cousin Joel was a bully who selfishly took the best holiday treats for himself. Jesus learned about compassion, kindness, and forgiveness, among other lessons, from his extended family, not only from his parents. Overlooking offenses is an important skill for family tranquility. Maybe an older cousin teased Jesus about being a man when he turned twelve. What have my family members taught me—valuable lessons that I didn't want to learn?

1 Samuel 1:20–22,24–28 or Sirach 3:2–6,12–14
Psalm 84:2–3,5–6,9–10 or Ps 128:1–2, 3, 4–5
1 John 3:1–2,21–24 or Colossians 3:12–21 or 3:12–17
Luke 2:41–52

DECEMBER 27

• ST. JOHN, APOSTLE AND EVANGELIST •

[F]or the life was made visible;
we have seen it and testify to it
and proclaim to you the eternal life
that was with the Father and was made visible to us
—1 JOHN 1:2

I am an eyewitness of Jesus at work. You are too. Whenever love manifests in deeds, God is laboring with us. My heart burns with excitement when I realize that I have touched God in the people around me. God is as close as the human being nearest to you right now. Every person is an image of the mighty God. When we worship together and when we talk about our faith, we are openly proclaiming the fantastic news that God's Word lives tangibly among us. We, too, have seen and heard the Lord.

1 John 1:1–4
Psalm 97:1–2,5–6,11–12
John 20:1a,2–8

If we say, "We are without sin,"
we deceive ourselves, and the truth is not in us.
—1 JOHN 1:8

When good people don't do what we expect them to do, we
may react angrily, taking actions we later regret. Feeling
angry isn't a sin, but expressing rage in actions and fomenting
fury are destructive. We also face temptations *not* to act: not
to forgive, not to let go of hurt, and not to reach out to
someone who has deceived us. Grudges grow from next to
nothing sometimes. We pretend to forget, yet fury boils
within. We mask it, pretending nothing is wrong. It has the
same effect as ingesting poison and hoping someone else will
suffer from it. This is not what God wants for us.

1 John 1:5—2:2
Psalm 124:2–3,4–5,7b–8
Matthew 2:13–18

DECEMBER 29

• ST. THOMAS BECKET, BISHOP AND MARTYR •

It had been revealed to him by the Holy Spirit
that he should not see death
before he had seen the Christ of the Lord.
—LUKE 2:26

How did God reveal this to Simeon? How did Simeon know
the insight wasn't just his imagination? Perhaps Simeon
invested time in a prayer life of many years, which created a
"secure" communication channel where feelings of peace led
him to insights. Maybe he expected God to be in conversation
with him. Simeon's faith allowed him to look for God's
revealed truths in his life. He must have tested his perceptions
against several criteria, including his reason, the feedback of
other people, and prayerful intuition. Anna the prophetess was
a confirmation that Simeon's intuition was correct.

1 John 2:3–11
Psalm 96:1–2a,2b–3,5b–6
Luke 2:22–35

DECEMBER 30

Do not love the world or the things of the world.
—1 JOHN 2:15

The antique shop was full of dusty dishware, once valued so highly that the family never ate off it. At the octogenarian's demise, no one wanted it. The store also displayed full curio cabinets, vintage furniture, musty books, and fashions long out of style. Dusting was a major chore. What earthly treasures do you hoard or hold dear? Are they necessary to your happiness? What would it take to give ten things away today? Is your relationship with God so strong that you resist spending resources on things that don't last? Some souls are cluttered with unhelpful habits and ways of thinking. Others store loving relationships long past. Look into your soul as if it were a secondhand shop. Would people eagerly long to shop there, or would they pass by?

1 John 2:12–17
Psalm 96:7–8a,8b–9,10
Luke 2:36–40

Friday

DECEMBER 31

• ST. SYLVESTER I, POPE •

Thus we know this is the last hour.
—1 JOHN 2:18

Time to check my attitude about the last day of another year.
I experienced some sadness, loss, and unfinished business.
Time feels like a carpet ripped from under me, and I wonder
how the month disappeared so quickly. The epistle writer
today tells us that we are in the last days. If this is true,
perhaps I will pray to better prioritize this day. It may be the
only day left to me. None of us ever knows. Dear God, help
us rise to greet a new year with hope and priorities reoriented
toward you. Thank you for forgiving and offering a clean
slate again. Help me focus on the good things and to give
you thanks. With your help, I look forward to a fresh start.

1 John 2:18–21
Psalm 96:1–2,11–12,13
John 1:1–18

The LORD look upon you kindly
and give you peace!
—NUMBERS 6:26

The Catholic Church first celebrated a World Day of Peace in January 1968. Over the years, popes have used the feast to make declarations of social doctrine. The world always seems to be in dire need of peace. I learned the hymn "Let There Be Peace on Earth" in fifth grade, and I can still hear our young voices belting out, "With every step I take, let this be my solemn vow: to take each moment, and live each moment in peace eternally!" God pierced my childish heart in a long-lasting moment of consolation and desire. What's your music memory like? Is there a song you hear that evokes a strong memory or emotion of peace?

Numbers 6:22–27
Psalm 67:2–3,5,6,8 (2a)
Galatians 4:4–7
Luke 2:16–21

Sunday

JANUARY 2

• THE EPIPHANY OF THE LORD •

Rise up in splendor, Jerusalem! Your light has come,
the glory of the LORD shines upon you.
—ISAIAH 60:1

Think about center stage, where a spotlight transforms pitch
darkness into a bright light on the performer. The crowd
cheers. God, the great director, shines the limelight upon
you! Or think about how it feels when hot sun heats your
skin on a blazing summer day. Be overwhelmed by the
scrutiny of brilliant love—of our God, who cares little about
failures and defeats. Hear Isaiah, who tells us to look around
and to see that others are also bathing in this luxurious light
of God's glory. You're not alone on this shore or in the
spotlight. Darkness flees. God's mercy and love pour upon
you like the penetrating sun of a blazing day.

Isaiah 60:1–6
Psalm 72:1–2,7–8,10–11,12–13
Ephesians 3:2–3a,5–6
Matthew 2:1–12

JANUARY 3

• THE MOST HOLY NAME OF JESUS •

*Beloved, do not trust every spirit
but test the spirits to see whether they
belong to God.*
—1 JOHN 4:1

Whose influence do we follow? Friends, relatives, and
strangers can nudge our actions. So can invisible forces. When
discouragement arrives, the negative takes the wheel and can
steer us off the highway of love. Suddenly the road is full of
ruts. While following Christ does not guarantee the absence of
potholes, we know that God's consolations navigate us to
Christ. God directs us toward greater faith, hope, love, and
peace. If those graces are running on empty, it's time to stop
and back up. Where did we take an off-ramp that left us listless
and created noisy turmoil? Look under the hood. Test the
energy levels. Reset the GPS (G for *God*) using more prayer,
and giving thanks when consolations finally return.

1 John 3:22—4:6
Psalm 2:7bc–8,10–12a
Matthew 4:12–17,23–25

Tuesday

JANUARY 4

• ST. ELIZABETH ANN SETON, RELIGIOUS •

"Give them some food yourselves."
—MARK 6:37

The patron of Catholic education took these words to heart. She fed students with loving instruction. It was the belief in Jesus as real food in the Eucharist that propelled St. Elizabeth Ann's conversion to Catholicism after losing her husband when she was thirty. You and I are called to give food to others, not only by donating literal food but also by feeding encouraging words, engaging in uplifting conversations, and providing a compassionate ear that listens without judgment or interruption. Jesus invites you and me to give the food that we have been given: our very lives, talents, and gifts. Does it seem like a meager portion? No worries. The measure of graces we have will be enough, with God's help, to build up the reign of God.

1 John 4:7–10
Psalm 72:1–2,3–4,7–8
Mark 6:34–44

Wednesday

JANUARY 5

• ST. JOHN NEUMANN, BISHOP •

He came toward them, walking on the sea.
He meant to pass by them.
—MARK 6:48

Don't think Jesus didn't understand being busy. He pulled an all-nighter of prayer after preaching all day, healing, and working miracles, and all of this while grief-stricken at the recent news of John the Baptist's death. Imagine what that was like. He needed more time! Perhaps he didn't want his followers to know how he was trying to squeeze more into his day, and that's why he was going to pass their boat, miraculously walking on water. Maybe he had a more compassionate reason or he didn't want to reveal his divinity so obviously just yet. When feeling too busy and wanting to cheat the clock, turn to Jesus, who understands because he experienced the same feelings as we do.

1 John 4:11–18
Psalm 72:1–2,10,12–13
Mark 6:45–52

Thursday

JANUARY 6

• ST. ANDRÉ BESSETTE, RELIGIOUS •

Beloved, we love God because
he first loved us.
—1 JOHN 4:19

Love is like a Möbius strip: there's only one side—the loving
one. God loves first, which leads people into loving. God
communicates love to the beloved, and the beloved, in
return, reciprocates to the lover. God is present whenever
love is active. To be genuinely loved is so attractive that it's
difficult to resist. And when loving someone, it's much easier
to sacrifice a personal agenda for theirs. We belong to God
whenever we enter the mystery of loving. Before long, love is
looping back from some divine source. Love doesn't originate
in humanity; love is a free gift from God. And it's infinite.

1 John 4:19—5:4
Psalm 72:1–2,14 and 15bc,17
Luke 4:14–22a

Friday

JANUARY 7

• ST. RAYMOND OF PENYAFORT, PRIEST •

He would withdraw to deserted places to pray.
—LUKE 5:16

Miracle stories and parables are told and retold. But quiet prayers don't have such great publicity. Jesus often made concerted efforts to get in quiet prayer time. When people have busy agendas, the temptation to scrap alone-with-God time rises. Jesus prioritized prayer. He had many of the same challenges that people face in modern society. While introverts thrive on time alone, extroverts can turn squirrelly with too much solitude. Finding balance is important. Prayer time will be as unique as each individual. Prayer is relationship, and it's pretty difficult to build a relationship when only one person talks all the time or when one never listens. Was Jesus an extrovert or an introvert, or a perfect integration of both? Did he crave more quiet or company?

1 John 5:5–13
Psalm 147:12–13,14–15,19–20
Luke 5:12–16

Now a dispute arose between the disciples
of John and a Jew
about ceremonial washings.
—JOHN 3:25

Sometimes people argue about what they later discover to be
small stuff. It seems so important at the time. A relationship
may be permanently damaged, and years later the people
cannot even remember why they disagreed. Relationships
require work, patience, and humility. People close to us can
misunderstand, misconstrue, and misinterpret our intentions,
and that's in addition to the mistakes we can make in relation
to them. Egos get involved, as it seems they did in today's
Gospel. It's human to get upset with another person's
behavior. What does it take to forgive, overlook a difference,
and assume the best intentions from the other?

1 John 5:14–21
Psalm 149:1–2,3–4,5 and 6a and 9b
John 3:22–30

Sunday

JANUARY 9

• THE BAPTISM OF THE LORD •

The grace of God has appeared, saving all
and training us to reject godless ways
and worldly desires.
—TITUS 2:11

It's only the ninth, and New Year's resolutions may have
faltered already. Time to rededicate ourselves to those loving
habits already in place. God's grace is alive and active. Don't
forget to ask for it. It's possible to grow incrementally and
accept a fresh start every day. One way to cooperate with
grace is to write life mission statements. For instance, I live to
be in relationship with God through Jesus. I strive to be
motivated by love, not money. I want the world to be a
better place because I was here. I deserve to feel good about
myself; I am an image of God. I will leave the earth cleaner
than I found it.

Isaiah 40:1–5,9–11 or Isaiah 42:1–4, 6–7
Psalm 104:1b–2,3–4,24–25,27–28,29–30 (1) or Ps 29:1–2, 3–4, 3, 9–10
Titus 2:11–14; 3:4–7 or Acts 10:34–38
Luke 3:15–16,21–22

JANUARY 10

The cup of salvation I will take up,
and I will call upon the name of the LORD.
—PSALM 116:13

What do you do when you're feeling terrible—not
necessarily sick, but discouraged, down, or generally
disappointed in yourself or others? Everyone has days like
this: prayer feels like sawdust, God seems distant, and staying
in bed is more attractive than getting to work. Spiritual
leaders throughout history have given this advice: pray more.
A rote prayer helps, even if it feels empty. Try repeating,
"Jesus! Help!" Turn on music or sing a hymn whose words
redirect the mood. You will probably feel like these are the
last things you want to do. Do them anyway. Tell yourself
that you will get through this. Negative forces want you to
stay down or to make radical changes (like moving to Tahiti
or quitting a job). Make an act of will; you are *not* alone.

1 Samuel 1:1–8
Psalm 116:12–13,14–17,18–19
Mark 1:14–20

JANUARY 11

In her bitterness she prayed to the LORD,
weeping copiously.
—1 SAMUEL 1:10

I wish I could rewind a day and get more out of it. I am not a big fan of Mondays, when everything seems a little drearier after I've enjoyed some needed Sabbath rest and uplifting worship with our community on Sunday. I'm tempted to feel let down when beginning a new work week. Here it is Tuesday already, and I still have a list of unfinished business from Monday. I put a sticky note on yesterday's reflection so I can return to it later when I simply cannot remember what to do in desolate times. Today I pray the Serenity Prayer, the longer version, which includes the line, "living one day at a time . . . accepting hardship as a pathway to peace."

1 Samuel 1:9–20
1 Samuel 2:1,4–5,6–7,8abcd
Mark 1:21–28

JANUARY 12

*I have waited, waited for the LORD,
and he stooped toward me and heard my cry.*
—PSALM 40:2

Be patient, St. Ignatius advises in his eighth rule for discerning spirits. When we are in desolation, patience is a counterattack, he said. Wait this trial out; tomorrow will soon arrive and with it, the promise of a new day. Perseverance doesn't seem very proactive. But experience taught the pilgrim, as St. Ignatius called himself, that waiting was a great strategy. His years as a soldier come through here; isn't patience a form of "soldiering on"? He also advised prayer, penance, and pondering the choices made that got the directee here. Things will be better, tomorrow. God's encouragement will return eventually.

1 Samuel 3:1–10,19–20
Psalm 40:2 and 5,7–8a,8b–9,10
Mark 1:29–39

JANUARY 13

• ST. HILARY, BISHOP AND DOCTOR OF THE CHURCH •

A leper came to him and kneeling down
begged him and said,
"If you wish, you can make me clean."
—MARK 1:40

The worst case is not as bad as the fear and anxiety of anticipating it. If someone had predicted how things would change a year before COVID-19 became a pandemic, people may have succumbed to anticipatory fear. As communities lived through it, people received graces to make it to the world as we know it now. Jesus takes pity on us when we're suffering, and he doesn't mind if we beg for strength to push through life's difficulties. "I do will your healing," he says. He wants to be asked for God's intervention in our lives. In story after story, Jesus asks people what they want from him. We must never be hesitant to ask.

1 Samuel 4:1–11
Psalm 44:10–11,14–15,24–25
Mark 1:40–45

JANUARY 14

*When Jesus returned to Capernaum after some days,
it became known that he was at home.*
—MARK 2:1

Approximately thirty miles from Nazareth, Capernaum sits
on the edge of the sea of Galilee. Perhaps Jesus moved there
during his private life, taking Mary to live with him after his
dad died. Near the water he could obtain carpentry work on
boats. What was it like when Jesus was at home? Do you
picture him living alone and having customers come to him
for woodworking jobs? Allow yourself to walk in your
imagination down to the edge of the sea with Jesus. The
weather is temperate and dry. Perhaps you see a turtle, a
further invitation to slow down. Talk to Jesus about your own
home. Think about what Jesus might ask you to change.
Ponder, as his mother taught him to do by her example.

1 Samuel 8:4–7,10–22a
Psalm 89:16–17,18–19
Mark 2:1–12

Saturday

JANUARY 15

You have granted him his heart's desire;
you refused not the wish of his lips.
—PSALM 21:3

The garden coordinator at the nonprofit stands in a driveway
at a table piled with fresh produce. Low-income neighbors
drop by for a few free items. A donor walks up with oranges,
refusing thanks; they came from a neighbor's overloaded tree.
A child quickly grabs one. Her mother smiles as juice runs
down the child's chin. One person's excess fulfills another's
wish. Neighbors organized to make this possible. A small act
of sharing fruit rippled outward. God invites those with
much to share with others. Grace flourishes. What can be
given away today to meet the desire of another's heart? What
can be offered today, beyond the excess with which people
so easily part?

1 Samuel 9:1–4,17–19; 10:1a
Psalm 21:2–3,4–5,6–7
Mark 2:13–17

JANUARY 16

• SECOND SUNDAY IN ORDINARY TIME •

You shall be a glorious crown in the hand of the LORD.
—ISAIAH 62:3

One thing I love about page-a-day books is that it's fine to simply move directly to today's date. If I miss a few days, it's okay. God knows where to find me even when *I* don't know where to find me. I don't need to catch up on days I missed. I move to and read today's reflection, ruminate about its thoughts, and allow peace to fill this moment. After all, I am a beautiful, jeweled treasure, worthy of display in a museum, and God holds me in a comfortably warm and gentle grip.

Isaiah 62:1–5
Psalm 96:1–2,2–3,7–8,9–10 (3)
1 Corinthians 12:4–11
John 2:1–11

JANUARY 17

• ST. ANTHONY, ABBOT •

The days will come when the bridegroom
is taken away from them,
and then they will fast.
—MARK 2:20

Christmas decorations may not even be put away, and we get
a foreshadowing of days to come: Lent will be here before
we know it. We will leave off meat on Fridays and take on
penitential acts. But is our bridegroom *ever* taken away from
us, really? Not when his name is Emmanuel, God-with-us.
He is with us in Eucharist as often as we want to make time
for its reception. He is a simple prayer away.

1 Samuel 15:16–23
Psalm 50:8–9,16bc–17,21 and 23
Mark 2:18–22

JANUARY 18

"Do not judge from his appearance."
—1 SAMUEL 16:7

The puzzle has 999 pieces all assembled, and it's a beautiful picture. But the eye gravitates to the hole. Where is that one piece? People often judge by what they see, obsess over a small flaw, and find themselves stuck in judgment or refusal to forgive and let go. Why focus on failings instead of seeing the many meaningful pieces that God created? It's impossible to know what's in someone else's mind. God looks within and loves all, even those with great big gaps and missing pieces. It is grace at work to assume the best of intentions from another person and to judge others less.

1 Samuel 16:1–13
Psalm 89:20,21–22,27–28
Mark 2:23–28

*The Pharisees went out and immediately took counsel
with the Herodians against [Jesus] to put him to death.*
—MARK 3:6

You may have heard a version of this saying attributed to
Ralph Waldo Emerson: when you sow a thought, you reap an
action; sow an action and you reap a habit; sow a habit and
you reap a character; sow a character and you reap a destiny.
It all begins with a thought. The Pharisees suspected Jesus
and reaped a pattern of condemnation. They sought out and
collected evidence to support their preconceived ideas. Such
behaviors lead to brokenness today also. But nothing can fix
our hurting world except the saving power of Jesus. Oh,
God! Send new hope today.

1 Samuel 17:32–33,37,40–51
Psalm 144:1b,2,9–10
Mark 3:1–6

*[Jesus] told his disciples to have a boat ready for him
because of the crowd,
so that they would not crush him.*
—MARK 3:9

Can you imagine Jesus planning an escape route from a
crowd so pressing that it might cause him physical harm? If
you were to put yourself in this story, would you be a disciple
hustling for a boat? You may express willingness to serve
Jesus at all costs and rush straight off, but it could be a tough
assignment. Or today do you feel like someone so ill that you
would be among those pushing to get closer to Jesus? Does
Jesus seem unaware of your suffering? Perhaps you are
shoving your way through to get a definitive answer to a
problem, forgetting about those around you as you press
forward with your own agenda.

1 Samuel 18:6–9; 19:1–7
Psalm 56:2–3,9–10a,10b–11,12–13
Mark 3:7–12

Friday

JANUARY 21

• ST. AGNES, VIRGIN AND MARTYR •

In the shadow of your wings I take refuge,
til harm pass by.
—PSALM 57:2

Winter strips the trees down to trunks, twigs, and branches.
Now it's easy to see straight through the forest. Every twist
and turn in the path is revealed. Leaves are luscious
obstructionists. Here is a metaphor for suffering. When I am
surrounded by the beauty of consolations, it's easy to stay
where I am, enjoying its fruits. But I am not called to worship
the consolations, but rather the God who provides them,
despite my unworthiness. I grow through adversity; when the
consolations fall away, it's easier to see beyond. Hardships
can lead to clearer vision and a call to serve others.

1 Samuel 24:3–21
Psalm 57:2,3–4,6 and 11
Mark 3:13–19

"I grieve for you, Jonathan my brother!
most dear you have been to me."
—2 SAMUEL 1:26

At the 2020 March for Life in Washington, D.C., participants carried a wide range of banners and viewpoints. The ones I remember most were signs saying, "I regret my abortion." The marchers, male, and female, walked with silent, serious faces. I was sidelined by the throng, but now I ran from my spot on the curb into the crowd and made eye contact with one of the women. "We love you," I said and hugged her on behalf of all who feel as I do. Struck by their bravery and wounded by their pain, I began walking again, feeling more sober about the task of publicly taking a stand for the dignity of all human life.

2 Samuel 1:1–4,11–12,19,23–27
Psalm 80: 2–3,5–7
Mark 3:20–21

JANUARY 23

• THIRD SUNDAY IN ORDINARY TIME •

If one part suffers, all the parts suffer with it;
if one part is honored, all the parts share its joy.
—1 CORINTHIANS 12:26

Lean on one another. It's like a stack of building blocks. If you pull out one of the base blocks, all the pieces will fall. The family of Christ is connected even though we feel separate at times. We have the power (stronger than we realize) to influence one another for good or ill. Like bean plants growing near one another, we send out tentative tendrils, hoping by probing to connect. When we do, those connections make us stronger while helping our neighbors, too.

Nehemiah 8:2–4a,5–6,8–10
Psalm 19:8,9,10,15
1 Corinthians 12:12–30 or 12:12–14, 27
Luke 1:1–4; 4:14–21

"No one can enter a strong man's house
to plunder his property
unless he first ties up the strong man.
—MARK 3:27

You sometimes see homes with intimidating iron fences
around them, with multiple locks on the front doors, and
signs alerting you that they have alarm systems installed.
What's inside must be pretty important. Jesus uses the
well-protected home as a metaphor for your soul and the
tactics evil uses. When you allow yourself to be bullied by
evil, it's as if you've been hog-tied and your mortal enemy is
entering the house. Spiritual freedom disappears when you
let nagging cravings and attachments tie you down.

2 Samuel 5:1–7,10
Psalm 89:20,21–22,25–26
Mark 3:22–30

Tuesday

JANUARY 25

• THE CONVERSION OF ST. PAUL THE APOSTLE •

The reply came, "I am Jesus, whom you are persecuting."
—ACTS 9:5

Sometimes the voice of God is so clear that no discernment is required. These moments are not as rare as they may seem, and not only famous saints have them. Spending time regularly in prayer makes people sensitive to God's quiet presence and leading. It's also true that if we're traveling on the wrong road, God is capable of intervening and stopping any progress toward a poor choice. God can be noisy when necessary. God knows how to reach individuals. When hearing nothing from God, select a course of action. Having used the various tools for discernment and prayed while feeling at peace, make the best choice via reason. Leave anxiety behind. Watch for confirmation. God can put a halt to things as he did for St. Paul.

Acts 22:3–16 or 9:1–22
Psalm 117:1bc,2
Mark 16:15–18

*Stir into flame
the gift of God that you have through the
imposition of my hands.
For God did not give us a spirit of cowardice
but rather of power and love and self-control.*
—2 TIMOTHY 1:6

The barbecue's coals were greying with ash. A quick stir
returned their bright red glow, and soon our marshmallows
were toasting. Wherein am I called to stir tepid gifts back
into a passionate glow? Flames quickly catch other things on
fire, too. My courage sometimes hides under ashes of fear,
but it is still there. The enemy of our human nature enjoys
dampening our spirits with petty pursuits. Yet God gave me a
sound mind and a command to love. I need never be
ashamed of letting my God-given gifts shine brightly.

2 Timothy 1:1–8 or Titus 1:1–5
Psalm 96:1–2a,2b–3,7–8a,10
Mark 4:1–20

JANUARY 27

• ST. ANGELA MERICI, VIRGIN •

*"Who am I, Lord GOD, and who are
the members of my house,
that you have brought me to this point?"*
—2 SAMUEL 7:18B

As a spiritual director, I am privileged to listen as people share their intimate conversations with God. I sometimes wonder, "Who am I to be in this role?" People often "hear" God wordlessly. One person "saw" Christ on the cross with his head turned, looking at her. She wondered if God really was communicating personally. "God 'speaks' all the time," I said. "Why not return to that image in prayer right now?" After some time, she said, "I see Christ's hand reaching out to me, in invitation, in a calling," she confirmed. "I feel peace." Following Christ isn't easy because Jesus sometimes beckons us to join him on the cross. I marveled at what I'd just witnessed.

2 Samuel 7:18–19,24–29
Psalm 132:1–2,3–5,11,12,13–14
Mark 4:21–25

Friday

JANUARY 28

• ST. THOMAS AQUINAS, PRIEST AND DOCTOR OF THE CHURCH •

*This is how it is with the Kingdom of God;
it is as if a man were to scatter seed on the land
and would sleep and rise night and day
and the seed would sprout and grow;
he knows not how.*
—MARK 4:27

Picture God as a gardener, liberally throwing seeds across a wide, well-tilled field. Some will be flowers and others vegetables. See yourself as that field. Imagine God's grace lavishly spreading over you. What does God hope to see growing soon? Have you made time to discern what God has planted? How will seeds burst forth if you don't allow God's living water and mercy to pour upon you? Jesus explains things very personally. As you watch for God's explanations, consider planting a good word somewhere.

2 Samuel 11:1–4a,5–10a,13–17
Psalm 51:3–4,5–6a,6bcd–7,10–11
Mark 4:26–34

JANUARY 29

A clean heart create for me, O God,
and a steadfast spirit renew within me.
—PSALM 51:12

Discernment between two good things is tough when we're attached to intractable ideas, expectations, anxiety, or fear. God is a house cleaner who comes to tidy up our hearts and free us from such messes. She brings her broom, moves the furniture, and wipes away dust bunnies, cobwebs, and worse. She labors to detach the dirt that clouds our judgment. God's spirit can shine when we invite in the divine janitor. Through God's intervention, our hearts are readied for company—for the best guest, Jesus.

2 Samuel 12:1–7a,10–17
Psalm 51:12–13,14–15,16–17
Mark 4:35–41

JANUARY 30

• FOURTH SUNDAY IN ORDINARY TIME •

[Jesus said,] "Today this Scripture passage is fulfilled in your hearing."
—LUKE 4:21

Jesus was the black sheep of Nazareth, not sticking to the plan the village had for him. When he came to share the good news of God's never-ending love, he was amazed at their lack of faith. Just the fact that they rejected him didn't mean he rejected them. Jesus loves even the black sheep among humanity. "Look," Jesus might have said, "I'm sending you to bring good news to people who are poor, suffering, and in need of healing. They are people in your own circle of influence, but they will reject you. It's okay! You're in good company. My company. God's Spirit rests upon you." This Scripture is fulfilled in 2022. Right now. Christ's Spirit rests with the church, even if people's reactions aren't exactly favorable.

Jeremiah 1:4–5,17–19
Psalm 71:1–2,3–4,5–6,15,17
1 Corinthians 12:31—13:13 or 13:4–13
Luke 4:21–30

JANUARY 31

• ST. JOHN BOSCO, PRIEST •

*[Jesus said,] "Go home to your family and announce to them
all that the Lord in his pity has done for you."*
—MARK 5:19

What a disappointment! I had great plans for traveling to
far-flung cities with Jesus and sharing my testimony—and he
sends me home! I felt . . . well, what do you think? Mad? Sad?
Humiliated? I wanted to continue the euphoria of standing
near Jesus. And yet, when I thought about it, going home
made perfect sense. My extended family needed me. I was
certainly no help during years of ranting in the tombs. Now
I'll witness to all who knew me when I was possessed. Before
heading to distant places, I'll care for those closest to me. I
was healed for a purpose: to be a blessing at home.

2 Samuel 15:13–14,30; 16:5–13
Psalm 3:2–3,4–5,6–7
Mark 5:1–20

FEBRUARY 1

*That day's victory was turned into mourning for
the whole army
when they heard that the king was grieving
for his son.*
—2 SAMUEL 19:3

How quickly we can go from heights of joy to pits of despair.
Grief welcomes companions, and it is a privileged place to
weep alongside another. My mother never asked what was
needed when someone in her parish suffered a death in the
household. She simply showed up at their front door with
food. This put the person opening the door in control. They
could say thanks, accept the gift, and close the door. Then
Mother knew they just needed to be alone. More often,
however, Mother was welcomed in for a visit in which she
listened to the stories that needed to be told. She was a
comfort just by being present. How do we mourn alongside
someone experiencing painful loss?

2 Samuel 18:9–10,14b,24–25a,30—19:3
Psalm 86:1–2,3–4,5–6
Mark 5:21–43

FEBRUARY 2

• THE PRESENTATION OF THE LORD •

Reach up, you ancient portals,
that the king of glory may come in!
—PSALM 24:9

Children stand a little taller when they are about to receive a
school or sports award. Their pride at the honor is visually
obvious. Similarly, the doorways of the temple lift themselves
higher to welcome for the first time the long-awaited
Messiah. The vulnerable baby enters, and creation celebrates.
Even inanimate gates react. Later, when it's his triumphal
entry into Jerusalem, Jesus will say that the very rocks will
cry out if people don't. Anna and Simeon were joyously
crying out when they recognized their Savior.

Malachi 3:1–4
Psalm 24:7,8,9,10
Hebrews 2:14–18
Luke 2:22–40

FEBRUARY 3

"Yours, O LORD, are grandeur and power,
majesty, splendor, and glory."
—1 CHRONICLES 29:11

Perhaps the earliest capital campaign in the Bible was King David's fundraising for the temple his son would build. In a speech right before today's passage from Chronicles, David describes what he has already stored up for the building project. He tells the leaders that he's donating his personal fortune. Then he asks, "Who'll join me?" The generosity of his people, who willingly donate, propels David into prayers of praise, used today as a responsorial. Seeing the generosity and self-sacrificing gifts of others often compels people to admiration and esteem for them. The wondrous God plants generosity in souls, and it's a grace meant to be shared.

1 Kings 2:1–4,10–12
1 Chronicles 29:10,11ab,11d–12a,12bcd
Mark 6:7–13

FEBRUARY 4

When [Herod] heard [John] speak, he was very much perplexed,
yet he liked to listen to him.
—MARK 6:20

Was God working on Herod's heart, bringing about a
conversion that never made it to fruition? Despite Herod's
choices, God sent a messenger to draw him back. Herod was
drawn to John like water on a sponge; John's words gently
pulled at him and left him longing to hear more. What would
have happened had Herodias not carried a grudge? What if
Herod had exhibited any courage to stand against the fear of
what others might think? God allowed everyone in this
scenario to exercise free will. Still, God hoped for outcomes
that would lead to conversion of hearts rather than
destructive grudges. Herod had the option to make a better
choice, and he could have opted to never put himself in such
a dreadful position in the first place.

Sirach 47:2–11
Psalm 18:31,47 and 50,51
Mark 6:14–29

FEBRUARY 5

• ST. AGATHA, VIRGIN AND MARTYR •

*"Come away by yourselves to a deserted place and
rest a while."*
—MARK 6:30

As the sun sets tonight, the Jewish people will begin their celebration of the Sabbath. Exodus includes the command, "Remember the sabbath day—keep it holy. Six days you may labor and do all your work, but the seventh day is a sabbath of the LORD." It's a time for religious observance and rest. Why is it so difficult to make time for these two important activities in 2022? "Sorry, God, no time for prayer; too much work to do." Jesus' mandate to leave a hectic life and rest for a while is an *invitation*. Come to the party! Rest with me. Prayer shouldn't feel like obligation; it's hanging out with a friend.

1 Kings 3:4–13
Psalm 119:9,10,11,12,13,14
Mark 6:30–34

FEBRUARY 6

• FIFTH SUNDAY IN ORDINARY TIME •

Likewise James and John, the sons of Zebedee,
who were partners of Simon.
—LUKE 5:10

Jesus called families. Simon Peter and Andrew were brothers
and business partners with another set of brothers who are
referenced in relationship to their father. Was Zebedee
known to Luke's readers, like when we say, "You know Mary,
the daughter of our parish secretary?" And don't forget Peter's
mother-in-law, who feeds the boys at her house after Jesus
cures her. Siblings can be teases, pains in the neck, and
closest friends for life. They tell the truth even when it's
uncomfortable and stand with each other even when they
disagree. Did Jesus think about this when he chose brothers
and perhaps his cousin to be apostles?

Isaiah 6:1–2a,3–8
Psalm 138:1–2,2–3,4–5,7–8 (1c)
1 Corinthians 15:1–11 or 15:3–8, 11
Luke 5:1–11

FEBRUARY 7

Let your faithful ones shout merrily for joy.
—PSALM 132:9

Weeks of waiting culminated in a great family reunion.
When we gathered at the meeting place, I jumped with
excitement to see so many loved ones. So did others: "How
long has it been?" This was it! The time I'd prepared for had
arrived. Relatives hugged and squealed. Children
immediately started games with one another. Joy was
unrestrained. It was hard to count; so many people attended.
All kinds of yummy comfort foods filled the tables. Perhaps
this is how I will feel when the saints greet us when we arrive
at last in heaven.

1 Kings 8:1–7,9–13
Psalm 132:6–7,8–10
Mark 6:53–56

FEBRUARY 8

• ST. JEROME EMILIANI, PRIEST• ST. JOSEPHINE BAKHITA, VIRGIN •

May your eyes watch night and day over this temple.
—1 KINGS 8:29

God dwells in our bodies, as in a temple. When I face physical limitations, God's temple seems in need of repair! St. Josephine Bakhita expressed gratitude to God for her suffering because it led her to Christ. Born in Darfur and sold into slavery at seven, this woman experienced many abuses, even torture, from a number of masters. Taken on a trip to Italy, she converted in 1890. Canossian Sisters pleaded her case in court, and she was freed. She became a Canossian Sister and was known for her deep sense of gratitude. She knew God was watching night and day over her through many dark years and believed adversity led her to Christ.

1 Kings 8:22–23,27–30
Psalm 84:3,4,5 and 10,11
Mark 7:1–13

Wednesday

FEBRUARY 9

Commit to the LORD your way;
trust in him, and he will act.
—PSALM 37:5

The child puts her hand in mine with such confidence and waits to be led. She has no fear. Trust is an attribute of children, and God invites me to imitate them. If I commit to walking in loving service, I may not have a smooth road, but I will be accompanied by Jesus, who can get me through the rocky parts. I need not fret or worry or stress or strain. God will take action and work all things out for good, even when it seems impossible that this could happen.

1 Kings 10:1–10
Psalm 37:30–31,39–40
Mark 7:14–23

FEBRUARY 10

• ST. SCHOLASTICA, VIRGIN •

[Jesus] entered a house and wanted no one to know about it.
—MARK 7:24

Whose house is this? I picture a roadside inn where, as the proprietor, I'm wiping down tables when a stranger walks in, looking tired and hungry. "May I help you?" I ask politely. "Thank you. I'll take whatever you're serving for lunch, and some water please." Something in his eyes compels me to want to comfort him. By the time I rush back from the kitchen, my inn is full of people. The man is shielding his face with a hand to his brow, but it's ineffectual; people are crowding around his table. This poor man! He seems to be as worn out as is humanly possible. People are clamoring to get something from him. He gives me a closed-mouthed grin and a thank-you. Whom have I just served?

1 Kings 11:4–13
Psalm 106:3–4,35–36,37 and 40
Mark 7:24–30

FEBRUARY 11

• OUR LADY OF LOURDES •

[Jesus] took him off by himself.
—MARK 7:33

In a movie about King George VI, who had a speech impediment, viewers graphically see the embarrassment and humiliation associated with not being able to speak a well-formed sentence. As a royal he suffered under expectations imposed upon him. Take a moment to consider a time when you faced embarrassment and humiliation. You most certainly didn't want an audience. When Jesus took the man with the speech impediment off by himself in the Gospel, he was withdrawing from curious onlookers. How great is the compassion of Jesus! Allow Jesus to heal your feelings around embarrassment and humiliation. Pray for the grace to be able to welcome ridicule, with Jesus, who suffered humiliation himself.

1 Kings 11:29–32; 12:19
Psalm 81:10–11ab,12–13,14–15
Mark 7:31–37

Saturday

FEBRUARY 12

[Jesus said,] "My heart is moved with pity for the crowd."
—MARK 8:2

Jesus feels deeply for those who follow him. He sees their need
and hunger. If I want to respond to the call of King Jesus, I need
to be willing to see the needs and hunger of others, too. Think
about a teacher who, feeling compassion for students
undergoing rigorous tests, sends them to recess. A widow
cooks for an ill neighbor who recently had surgery. Her pity
results in loving action. Are these imitations of Christ's
behavior? Jesus turns his compassionate human emotions into
service to the physical needs of the crowd. Who elicits feelings
of pity from me in the world today? If I hold a leadership
position, am I aware of the needs of those in my care?

1 Kings 12:26–32; 13:33–34
Psalm 106:6–7ab,19–20,21–22
Mark 8:1–10

FEBRUARY 13

Blessed is the one who trusts in the LORD.
—JEREMIAH 17:7

Blessings! A Jesuit friend years ago taught me to close emails with this wish. Jesus tells us we are blessed; the Beatitudes are a constant call to bless and be blessed. Gratitude is wrapped up in this. We are blessed like trees planted near running water, whose leaves never fade. We are blessed when we imitate Christ. Joy grows as a result. We are blest when we do everything for the praise and service of God. Peace bubbles up. Go forward today with blessings, and bless.

Jeremiah 17:5–8
Psalm 1:1–2,3,4 and 6 (40:5a)
1 Corinthians 15:12,16–20
Luke 6:17,20–26

FEBRUARY 14

• ST. CYRIL, MONK, AND ST. METHODIUS, BISHOP •

Consider it all joy, my brothers and sisters,
when you encounter various trials,
for you know that the testing of your faith
produces perseverance.
—JAMES 1:2

The cross of Sts. Cyril and Methodius has a bar for Christ's footrest, as well as a bar above the one for his arms. In the icon of Mary, Mother of Perpetual Help, Jesus looks up at this Byzantine cross being presented to him by an angel, who is sent from the Creator to foreshadow Christ's demise even when he was a baby. Jesus shrinks back into the protection of his mother. No life is free of trials; strength to persevere can be found in the help of Mary's protective and loving arms.

James 1:1–11
Psalm 119:67,68,71,72,75,76
Mark 8:11–13

FEBRUARY 15

All good giving and every perfect gift is from above.
—JAMES 1:17

Our six-year-old grandson sent us a valentine. It gives me
such joy. I've kept it for a year in a place of honor. To see his
childish handwriting is so endearing—I love it even more
because he made the *D* backwards. It's the flaws that make it
spectacular. Here's a thought: that's how God feels about me.
God finds my shortcomings endearing. But when I become
aware of my mistakes, I want to eliminate all record of them.
I certainly don't love them. It's easy to judge myself harshly.

God sees all the love between the lines of my efforts. I
suspect my grandson will want me to throw away that
valentine someday, but I'll resist. It gives me courage to make
a valentine for God.

James 1:12–18
Psalm 94:12–13a,14–15,18–19
Mark 8:14–21

FEBRUARY 16

*Humbly welcome the word that has been
planted in you.*
—JAMES 1:21

Grace is personal. Two people visited Washington's National
Conservatory, an indoor space that mimics the tropics
despite a chill outside. One complained, "Is this all there is?"
The building is not that large. The other person marveled at
every flower, stopping frequently to enjoy staring at one
blossom and then another, noticing the differences. It led to
adoration of their Creator: a free grace, and the comment, "I
could stay here all day." The person complaining came to see
with new eyes as seeds of appreciation began to grow for
nature's diversity, even among humble manifestations.

James 1:19–27
Psalm 15:2–3a,3bc–4ab,5
Mark 8:22–26

FEBRUARY 17

• THE SEVEN HOLY FOUNDERS OF THE SERVITE ORDER •

"You are thinking not as God does,
but as human beings do."
—MARK 8:33

Poor Peter. You can almost hear him say, "Jesus, of course I'm thinking like a person! It's who I am!" Peter speaks to Jesus the way an intimate friend would; he shares his thoughts and opinions. What does Jesus expect? Perhaps it was his human side that rebuked Peter with such a remark. How puzzling that Jesus would knowingly walk into a trap, suffer greatly, and be killed. It's all part of the plan? Peter lacked Christ's divine perspective. It takes discernment to know when to suffer by standing firm and when to let something go. The noblemen who founded the Servites exhibited great courage when they left lucrative professions for austere lives of penance and prayer. They endeavored to think with God.

James 2:1–9
Psalm 34:2–3,4–5,6–7
Mark 8:27–33

Blessed [be] the man . . .who greatly delights in [the LORD's] commands.
—PSALM 112:1

Taco Tuesdays are a thing now. It started out small. Maybe Gratitude Fridays could go viral. The world could use encouragement to be more grateful. People could thank somebody for something—anything. It wouldn't have to be big. It could be, "Thank you for delivering the mail" or "Thanks for opening the door." People could express gratitude intentionally through social media, email, a phone call, or even with a rare mailed card. Getting a friendly postcard is really quite unusual. Every day offers countless opportunities to form the habit of thanking God. Will people jump on the bandwagon and spread a little joy by thanking God's people as well? And yes, "Thank God it's Friday!"

James 2:14–24,26
Psalm 112:1–2,3–4,5–6
Mark 8:34—9:1

Saturday

FEBRUARY 19

"This is my beloved Son. Listen to him."
—MARK 9:7

"I'm not sure I believe God speaks to me," a man told his
spiritual director. He wondered if imaginative thoughts
during contemplation were coming only from himself.
Director and directee examined the underlying feelings,
looking for peace, love, or an increase in hope. It appeared
that the man's faith in prayer was shaky. After a period of
silent listening, the man said, "I think God said, 'I know
you're trying. I'm here.' But that's not enough for me!" He
wanted a definitive answer, not encouragement. God allows
people to remain in a fog sometimes, giving little clues but
not opening the clouds and delivering clear messages. Yet
God speaks every day. Learning to listen without judgment is
a grace. It also involves being open to surprise.

James 3:1–10
Psalm 12:2–3,4–5,7–8
Mark 9:2–13

FEBRUARY 20

• SEVENTH SUNDAY IN ORDINARY TIME •

Love your enemies and do good to them.
—LUKE 6:35

This is the behavior that shows us to be children of the Most High; we follow in the footsteps of our Daddy, who is kind to the ungrateful and the undeserving. People have periods of ingratitude. Pity parties focus attention on self. But this doesn't mean folks stop needing and deserving love. God probably laughs with glee when watching our feeble attempts to love enemies. It's a laugh full of love and appreciation for humanity's efforts. Those who love as God loves have no enemies.

1 Samuel 26:2,7–9,12–13,22–23
Psalm 103:1–2,3–4,8,10,12–13 (8a)
1 Corinthians 15:45–49
Luke 6:27–38

FEBRUARY 21

Who among you is wise and understanding?
Let him show his works by a good life
in the humility that comes from wisdom.
—JAMES 3:13

When churches closed and Masses were cancelled during the pandemic that began in 2020, Pope Francis told priests to keep visiting the sick; prayers alone were insufficient. It was a call to follow the example of Father Damien, who put personal safety aside to serve people ostracized by everyone. He eventually died of leprosy. Finding the balance between helping others and risking death requires discernment. Do people depend upon you? How would they fare if you died during difficult circumstances? Martyrdom might involve not putting yourself at risk in order to sacrifice to the daily mundane tasks such as child or elder care. We need wisdom to decipher God's call.

James 3:13–18
Psalm 19:8,9,10,15
Mark 9:14–29

"Who do people say that the Son of Man is?"
—MATTHEW 16:13

St. Ignatius of Loyola called God "Divine Majesty." He knew what a king was like from his days at court. Isaiah called God wonderful counselor, mighty God, and prince of peace.

Other titles include miracle worker, promise keeper, everlasting love, light in the darkness, life giver, and gentle first truth (St. Catherine of Siena liked that one). There are many options for pet names to use when praying. What is your preferred name for God? When you picture talking to God, whom are you addressing? Creator, Healer, Beloved, Dear Brother, Spirit? Spend some time thinking about who you say God is and who God sees you to be. Who does your life say Christ is?

1 Peter 5:1–4
Psalm 23:1–3a,4,5,6
Matthew 16:13–19

"Whoever is not against us is for us."
—MARK 9:40

Christians use ambiguous terminology to establish common ground for faith discussions and prayer when they have denominational differences. In this way, connections are made without causing unnecessary offense. *Communion*, for example, means different things to Methodists and Lutherans. *Atonement* and *reconciliation* hold many shades of meaning. Even the Catholic Bible is different from a Protestant one (it has more Old Testament books, based on an early Judaic tradition of what was in the Hebrew Scriptures). People strive to make good moral choices even when their consciences are not fully formed. Jesus teaches inclusivity; Jesus connects people. Unity is possible even when differences are dramatic. The letter to the Romans offers another perspective on the same concept: "If God is for us, who can be against?"

James 4:13–17
Psalm 49:2–3,6–7,8–10,11
Mark 9:38–40

FEBRUARY 24

Jesus said to his disciples:
"Anyone who gives you a cup of water to drink
because you belong to Christ,
amen, I say to you, will surely not lose his reward."
—MARK 9:41

I heard a familiar word in the Gospel and thought, "Oh, yeah. I know this story." My mind drifted to my family, neighborhood, and activities. Then I was hearing, "The Gospel of the Lord." I joined the assembly: "Praise to you, Lord Jesus Christ," and sat down. What had just happened? I had tuned out, lost in my own thoughts and absent from the liturgy. Jesus, can I hit rewind? It doesn't work like that, does it? But I know God holds me, aware of all these distractions. And it's all okay. God loves unconditionally, whether I feel worthy or not.

James 5:1–6
Psalm 49:14–15ab,15cd–16,17–18,19–20
Mark 9:41–50

FEBRUARY 25

Do not complain, brothers and sisters,
about one another,
that you may not be judged.
—JAMES 5:9

We live in a world of people complaining. A negative word falls down a slippery slope, leading to more negativity. One unkind comment leads to, "Yeah, and also. . . ." The antidote to this is gratitude. When the overarching mood is a grateful one, it's much easier to overlook another person's shortcomings. It's best to encourage, not disparage. Not every misstep needs to be pointed out. An ungrateful heart slides into criticism. Before we know it, judgmental opinions are flying. Stop. (Dare to say that out loud.) Back up. "Now let's each say one positive remark about anything. Anyone." Watch the mood in the room change.

James 5:9–12
Psalm 103:1–2,3–4,8–9,11–12
Mark 10:1–12

FEBRUARY 26

The fervent prayer of a righteous person is very powerful.
—JAMES 5:16

My mother's prayers were powerful because of the faith that backed them up. She and my dad instilled in me a belief that I was loved so strongly that mountains could move. Sometimes I wonder who prayed for me when I didn't even know it, because I often pray for a face across the room. I remember being that mom several pews ahead struggling with a loud toddler. The other person in this doctor's waiting room needs a prayer. Who is praying for you right now? And who are you praying for, or could you be praying for, in this moment? You likely will never know how your prayer was heard. Someone desperately needs your faith right now. You share a loving secret with God when you pray for a stranger in your path today.

James 5:13–20
Psalm 141:1–2,3 and 8
Mark 10:13–16

FEBRUARY 27

• EIGHTH SUNDAY IN ORDINARY TIME •

The fruit of a tree shows the care it has had;
so too does one's speech disclose the bent of one's mind.
—SIRACH 27:6

People credit Mark Twain with having said, "Better to remain
silent and be thought a fool than to speak and remove all
doubt." Today's reading from Sirach originated this idea.
Speaking without thinking first often leads to regret. People
who speak to hear their own thoughts are familiar with
remorse. When hearts are rooted in love, words are less
likely to be harmful. A day that begins with prayer produces
better outcomes than a day without it. There are times when
the most loving option is to say nothing rather than voice a
criticism or downward-spiraling thought.

Sirach 27:4–7
Psalm 92:2–3,13–14,15–16
1 Corinthians 15:54–58
Luke 6:39–45

Great are the works of the LORD,
exquisite in all their delights.
—PSALM 111:2

We are God's unique creations, God's works of art. This psalm underscores the truth that the Almighty made us good and that God takes delight in us. Recognizing our creaturehood leads to gratitude welling up inside. We are beloved, exquisite, and made more beautiful by our flaws.

Kintsukuroi is a style of Japanese pottery that emphasizes broken places by filling them in with gold or silver. The repairs highlight cracks that didn't result in destruction. Our creative God brings beauty out of our scars if we allow it. Choose forgiveness, and let the wounds be filled by God with golden light. We are more precious and valued than we know. Is original sin the disparaging of self, saying, "I'm not good enough"?

1 Peter 1:3–9
Psalm 111:1–2,5–6,9 and 10c
Mark 10:17–27

*[Jesus said,] "Many that are first will be last,
and the last will be first."*
—MARK 10:31

Human nature gravitates toward pride. And from it, all kinds
of problems grow. Self-aggrandizement sneaks up while
people aren't paying attention. First, they succumb to the
temptation to prioritize money and stuff above people and
relationships. Then comes taking credit for achievements
that in reality are based on God-given talents. How easy it
becomes to forget to be grateful to God. Accepting
congratulations and honors for accomplishments is fine, as
long as God gets the praise, because credit is truly due to
God. "Me first" leads to riches, honors, and pride. Jesus never
sought these. He lived the opposite—humility—constantly.
God is comfortable with paradox.

1 Peter 1:10–16
Psalm 98:1,2–3ab,3cd–4
Mark 10:28–31

Wednesday

MARCH 2

• ASH WEDNESDAY •

Rend your hearts, not your garments,
and return to the LORD, your God.
—JOEL 2:12–13

In ancient times, people tore their clothes to broadcast intense emotion, particularly grief. Joel is asking people to skip the showy externals and convey heartfelt sorrow over their actions that have displeased God. Today the church invites us to reconsider our conversion's depth to see if we can move to more authentic discipleship. Is sorrow genuine, or are we habitually collecting ashes for display? We may not weep over sins because their significance and consequences are forgotten. Sins reject the generous gift of love personified. God is opulently merciful and willingly forgives when people admit their failures. God longs for us to return, not superficially, but genuinely thankful for another opportunity. May today be the start of something new: a reformed heart that seeks God in all things.

Joel 2:12–18
Psalm 51:3–4,5–6ab,12–13,14 and 17
2 Corinthians 5:20—6:2
Matthew 6:1–6,16–18

Choose life, then,
that you and your descendants may live,
by loving the LORD, your God.
—DEUTERONOMY 30:19–20

Although many people try to decipher God's will, it's not difficult to figure out. Nor do you need an expert to decode it. God's ideas for your life are not some static, preordained plan. Even from the earliest books in the Bible, the invitation to follow God's will is clear: choose to be loving. All you must do is use love as a measuring stick. You have a great deal of flexibility in your elected life path. Cooperate with love, discern what is the most caring action, and know that you are precious to a very personal God.

Deuteronomy 30:15–20
Psalm 1:1–2,3,4 and 6
Luke 9:22–25

Friday

MARCH 4

• FRIDAY AFTER ASH WEDNESDAY • ST. CASIMIR •

Sharing your bread with the hungry,
sheltering the oppressed and the homeless;
Clothing the naked when you see them.
—ISAIAH 58:7

When Jesus tells the parable of the sheep and goats in Matthew 25, it's not an original idea. About seven hundred years earlier, the prophet spoke of the sure way to see someone's light shine, and it had everything to do with serving one's neighbors, whether they be hungry, homeless, naked, or suffering any other need. When Jesus said that he came to fulfill the law and the prophets, here is a passage that explains how. The command is to unbind those detained unjustly and free those who are oppressed. No wonder it was tough to embrace the message of the Messiah when Jesus preached it. No wonder it's difficult today.

Isaiah 58:1–9a
Psalm 51:3–4,5–6ab,18–19
Matthew 9:14–15

And leaving everything behind, [Levi] got up and followed [Jesus].
—LUKE 5:28

Just like that, Levi turned his back on his post. It took two
words from Jesus. How many times does Jesus have to say,
"Follow me," before I drop everything? Right now, Jesus?
Really? What about all my commitments, meetings, and bills?
I've got lots to do this weekend, Jesus. What if I pray an hour
tomorrow? Right now I've got to catch up on chores, errands,
and my favorite TV show. Levi threw a big banquet. That
had to be costly. I'm on a budget, Jesus. I've already given my
donations for the month. My words begin to sound hollow
to me. I can sense that Jesus looks into my eyes with love and
invitation. I pray for the grace to let something go and
respond generously to Christ.

Isaiah 58:9b–14
Psalm 86:1–2,3–4,5–6
Luke 5:27–32

Sunday

MARCH 6

• FIRST SUNDAY OF LENT •

Because he clings to me, I will deliver him.
—PSALM 91:14

I have a spray to remove the sticky residue of white flies from
my prized gardenia bush. It works for a time. I need to be
vigilant because the flies keep coming back and making
themselves comfortably at home in that plant. My spirit needs
a similar spray. Temptations come after me like white flies. I
know that my sins are forgiven, but the memories of them
return, tempting me to beat myself up rather than turn to God
for continued release. Again I turn to God, asking for freedom
from the residue of my sins. I remember the promise that I will
be delivered. I'm invited to be thankful for that assurance.

Deuteronomy 26:4–10
Psalm 91:1–2,10–11,12–13,14–15
Romans 10:8–13
Luke 4:1–13

Monday

MARCH 7

• ST. PERPETUA AND ST. FELICITY, MARTYRS •

You shall love your neighbor as yourself.
—LEVITICUS 19:18

How well do we love ourselves? In a world that prizes individuality and self-sufficiency, we become self-absorbed, which is different from loving who we are. Proper eating, exercise, and rest are ways to love ourselves without being self-focused. So is turning away from nagging thoughts that tempt us to concentrate on wrongs and shortcomings in our world. Once we care for ourselves, we have something to give to someone else. Felicity and Perpetua grew close while imprisoned for following Jesus. They gave one another comfort as they awaited martyrdom. Perpetua was a well-educated noblewoman who nursed her child while imprisoned. Felicity gave birth in prison and gave her child to a Christian woman of Carthage. These women could do this because, first, they knew they were lovable and loved. Love would remain.

Leviticus 19:1–2,11–18
Psalm 19:8,9,10,15
Matthew 25:31–46

Tuesday

MARCH 8

• ST. JOHN OF GOD, RELIGIOUS •

"This is how you are to pray:"
—MATTHEW 6:9

I've got something I need to do. Instead, I straighten my desk, check text messages, and eliminate clutter. I recognize these avoidance behaviors. Perhaps I'm clearing my mind before tackling the tough job. The same thing happens in my prayer time. I pour coffee, jot a reminder for later, and list tasks to do. Then I take a deep breath and begin to pray. Oh! Do I have an appointment soon? I reach for the calendar, and right then my phone displays a text; soon I'm completely distracted. Is this avoidance behavior, or is God helping me clear my mind before I tackle the important job of spending time with my most beloved Friend? I think it's both. Before beginning prayer, take a deep breath and remember with whom you will speak.

Isaiah 55:10–11
Psalm 34:4–5,6–7,16–17,18–19
Matthew 6:7–15

Jonah began his journey through the city,
and had gone but a single day's walk announcing,
"Forty days more and Nineveh shall be destroyed,"
when the people of Nineveh believed God;
they proclaimed a fast
and all of them, great and small, put on sackcloth.
—JONAH 3:4–5

It was near this date two years ago that the World Health Organization declared COVID-19 a pandemic. People had no idea how the world would change. Uncertainty was everywhere. Plans were abandoned. Would this altered reality last a few weeks? What steps could stem the tide of illness and reduce the danger? New vocabulary, such as "social distancing," became commonplace. Fear erupted, and the common good of slowing the curve overtook people's minds. Behaviors changed. No one could predict the future. Sackcloth took on new meaning.

Jonah 3:1–10
Psalm 51:3–4,12–13,18–19
Luke 11:29–32

Thursday
MARCH 10

Queen Esther, seized with mortal anguish,
had recourse to the LORD.
—ESTHER C:12

The Jews celebrate the Feast of Purim on March 17 this year,
honoring Queen Esther's brave rescue of the nation from
annihilation under Haman, the Persian king's advisor. Today's
first reading is the only daily lectionary passage from the book
of Esther, which is read by Jews on Purim. Esther dared to
break accepted practice and approached the king, her
husband. No wonder she fasted and prayed with grief and
passion. She was taking her life in her hands. Smart woman:
she turned in prayer to the only one with the true power to
save her people. God's presence is refuge during suffering or
fear. Esther acknowledged her utter dependence on God by
praying, "Help me, who am alone and have no help but you,
Lord."

Esther C:12,14–16,23–25
Psalm 138:1–2ab,2cde–3,7c–8
Matthew 7:7–12

≥ 103 ≤

My soul waits for the LORD.
—PSALM 130:5

Really? Do we wait on the Lord, or do we barrel ahead and ask God to rubber-stamp our choices? Oh, sure, what we do is good. But is it really the best choice we could have made? We take over the wheel and put God in the passenger seat. God is still present as we speed along in a compromise rather than let Jesus drive. When St. Ignatius wrote a meditation on three kinds of people, he pointed to the procrastinator, who waits too long; the compromiser, who takes Jesus along for a ride but maintains control; and the one who waits on the Lord while praying and paying attention. God is faithful and loves to be asked. How can we better wait expectantly!

Ezekiel 18:21–28
Psalm 130:1–2,3–4,5–7a,7bc–8
Matthew 5:20–26

[Jesus said,] "So be perfect, just as your heavenly Father is perfect."
—MATTHEW 5:48

What's the difference between a plain white tile and marble?
One is affordable, and the other is expensive and highly
coveted. It's the flaws that make marble beautiful and costly.
Jesus knows humanity's weaknesses but invites people to
strive to be like God anyway. A plain white tile with no
marbling is not as precious as the work God creates by
incorporating cracks and colors. Each person is in process,
the result of God's creative artwork. God uses everything,
including our poor choices. Beauty and value shine through
the scars. Only God defines perfection.

Deuteronomy 26:16–19
Psalm 119:1–2,4–5,7–8
Matthew 5:43–48

Whom should I fear?
The LORD is my life's refuge;
of whom should I be afraid?
—PSALM 27:1

Walking one morning, I noticed that the bright sun elongated my shadow into an enormous version of myself, at least five times bigger than the real me. Evil tries to do the same thing: to make me focus on me-me-me and to exaggerate my problems to appear like giant specters much larger than my abilities to cope. That shadow suggests intimidating fear. But wait. All I had to do was to turn around. Helen Keller said, "Keep your face to the sunshine and you cannot see the shadow." I still have shortcomings, but my focus is on the Son, who bathes me in warmth and love. I put the shadow behind me and let God help with the rest.

Genesis 15:5–12,17–18
Psalm 27:1,7–8,8–9,13–14 (1a)
Philippians 3:17—4:1 or 3:20—4:1
Luke 9:28b–36

MARCH 14

Justice, O Lord, is on your side; we are shamefaced even to this day.
—DANIEL 9:7

You may relate to Daniel's admission of disobedience. To be fair, justice would be on God's side if you were reprimanded. Your mortal enemy would want you to fall into the traps of desolation and discouragement, collecting nuggets of negativity. The Gospel doesn't apply only to how you treat others. It applies to how you treat yourself. If you have trouble extending to yourself the mercy you show to others remember this: no more condemnation. God forgives extravagantly. You must, too. Take the steps you need to take to start fresh.

Daniel 9:4b–10
Psalm 79:8,9,11 and 13
Luke 6:36–38

*[Jesus said,] "Whoever exalts himself will be humbled;
but whoever humbles himself will be exalted."*
—MATTHEW 23:12

The tale began as follows: Hadrian tried to ingratiate himself
to the official. "Most excellent one," he began, but there was
a falseness in the accolade. Hadrian bowed deeply at the
waist, extending a flourish with his hand. It was embarrassing
to witness. "Don't call me that!" the official replied. "I don't
belong on a pedestal any more than you do." Hadrian felt
suitably humiliated, caught in the act of trying to earn points
with someone by using a fancy title. If only Hadrian had
embraced words from a well-known litany of humility: From
the desire of being praised, deliver me, oh Jesus. From the
fear of being ridiculed, deliver me, oh Jesus.

Isaiah 1:10,16–20
Psalm 50:8–9,16bc–17,21 and 23
Matthew 23:1–12

MARCH 16

[Jesus said,] "Behold, we are going up to Jerusalem,
and the Son of Man will be handed over."
—MATTHEW 20:18

Ken, a conscientious worker, suspected that something was wrong on the job. People whispered in the hall, making eye contact with him but saying nothing aloud to him. Ken kept doing his job to the best of his ability. Things went downhill. His boss called him into the office. "Explain how this report was completed," he said with an adversarial tone. Each day, the work environment felt more tense. Emails hinted that Ken was being written up unjustly. Ken recognized the signs. He predicted his job loss to his spouse: "I'm going to be handed over soon." Jesus understands what humanity goes through.

Jeremiah 18:18–20
Psalm 31:5–6,14,15–16
Matthew 20:17–28

Thursday

MARCH 17

• ST. PATRICK, BISHOP •

Then Abraham said,
"If they will not listen to Moses and the prophets,
neither will they be persuaded
if someone should rise from the dead."
—LUKE 16:31

People can miss the point. Ubiquitous clues are overlooked or ignored. In many places today, people wear green and act silly but forget the faith of the holy man behind the holiday. A hilarious card shows St. Patrick driving a station wagon full of snakes who complain, "Are we there yet? I'm hungry. I have to use the bathroom." It wouldn't be funny if you didn't know the legend about St. Patrick driving snakes out of Ireland. Your faith is no laughing matter, and God puts people along life's path to help guide the way. Signs all around point to Jesus, the Way. Pay attention and don't miss the off-ramp. "Are we there yet?"

Jeremiah 17:5–10
Psalm 1:1–2,3,4 and 6
Luke 16:19–31

Friday

MARCH 18

• ST. CYRIL OF JERUSALEM, BISHOP AND DOCTOR OF THE CHURCH •

They sold Joseph to the Ishmaelites
for twenty pieces of silver.
—GENESIS 37:28A

Jealousy grew as they discussed their dad's favorite son. "Here comes that master dreamer," the brothers said spitefully. Negativity breeds more negativity, and before they knew it, the brothers were all complicit in a murder plot and cover-up. A simple feeling of jealousy over an article of clothing, a multicolored cloak, became a wedge to crack open a greater sin. But it wasn't the coat, was it? It was the underlying preference a father showed for one son. The father didn't intend for his love and preference to lead to harm. Little things led to big things. Pharisees let small jealousies fester, too, and in time it led to Christ being sold for thirty pieces of silver.

Genesis 37:3–4,12–13a,17b–28a
Psalm 105:16–17,18–19,20–21
Matthew 21:33–43,45–46

Saturday

MARCH 19

• ST. JOSEPH, SPOUSE OF THE BLESSED VIRGIN MARY •

The angel of the Lord appeared to him in a dream.
—MATTHEW 1:20

Mary and I decided not to announce that our son was the Messiah. Who would believe it anyway? We kept a low profile, despite the harrowing adventures every parent faces. How could we predict what God would want from him and from us? We lived on faith. After our experience in Bethlehem, I was even more vigilant about protecting our son and living simply. Thank God for my dreams. Maybe you have dreams, too. I know God leads me through them. I was named for our ancestor who was a dreamer, too. His ability to interpret dreams for the Pharaoh saved Israel in a time of famine. Interesting that I, too, experienced migration to Egypt. Yes, my family experienced refugee status and migration firsthand.

2 Samuel 7:4–5a,12–14a,16
Psalm 89:2–3,4–5,27 and 29
Romans 4:13,16–18,22
Matthew 1:16,18–21,24a or Luke 2:41–51a

Sunday

MARCH 20

• THIRD SUNDAY OF LENT •

*[God said,] "Remove the sandals from your feet,
for the place where you stand is holy ground."*
—EXODUS 3:5

To protect the carpets, we take off our shoes near the front
door. I don't think about it, but our home is holy ground.
Here is the place where our matrimonial sacrament is lived
out—a sure sign of God's love in the world. I walk on holy
ground in other people's homes, too. Think about times
when you take off your shoes. At the beach we shed our
shoes to enjoy warm sand between our toes and the zing of
cool water. Enjoyment of creation rises from our feet up as
we relax at the shore. Right before bed, my slippers come off.
Holy ground is all around. Wherever you are right now, as a
child of God, you stand on holy ground.

Exodus 3:1–8a,13–15 or 17:3–7
Psalm 103:1–2,3–4,6–7,8,11 (8a) or 95:1–2,6–7,8–9
1 Corinthians 10:1–6,10–12 or Romans 5:1–2,5–8
Luke 13:1–9 or John 4:5–42

Athirst is my soul for God, the living God.
When shall I go and behold the face of God?
—PSALM 42:3

Imagine the widow, coughing and parched, not wanting to give up. Three and a half years without rain in Sidon caused unbearable thirsts and withered crops. Soon she and her son would die, she thought. Her mouth was as dry as the desert. Death would be easier, she pondered, knowing she would see her God. Listen to her praying today's psalm. When Elijah the prophet arrived, she obeyed his request. Faith gave her generosity. Jesus longed to find such virtue and thirst among the residents of his hometown. If only they knew that Living Water stood before them. Jesus used the widow as an example of the ways God blessed Gentiles when his own people rejected God's prophets. God thirsts for humanity even now.

2 Kings 5:1–15b or Exodus 17:1–7
Psalms 42:2,3; 43:3,4 or 95:1–2, 6–7ab, 7c–9
Luke 4:24–30 or John 4:5–42

MARCH 22

Peter approached Jesus and asked him,
"Lord, if my brother sins against me,
how often must I forgive him?"
—MATTHEW 18:21

"My good opinion once lost is lost forever," says Mr. Darcy in Jane Austen's *Pride and Prejudice*. It's a fault he corrects by the end of the novel, forgiving the foibles of his intended's dysfunctional family. Prejudices stop people from reconsidering opinions or changing their minds, even when new evidence appears. Peter's question points to a belief that forgiveness had limits. Roadblocks between siblings or neighbors must have existed in Peter's day. Pride can prevent a willingness to let things go, setting limits such as, "The other person needs to apologize first." Where is this attitude present today?

Daniel 3:25,34–43
Psalm 25:4–5ab,6 and 7bc,8–9
Matthew 18:21–35

Wednesday

MARCH 23

• ST. TORIBIO DE MOGROVEJO, BISHOP •

Glorify the LORD, O Jerusalem;
praise your God, O Zion.
—PSALM 147:12

Glenn was overcome with gratitude and praise to God when
he found the very small key sandwiched between the sofa
cushions. Without it, his 3300-pound car was going
nowhere. The key was a big deal. The Israelites believed that
the key to their covenant was obedience to a set of statutes.
But Jesus, called the Key of David, unlocked the entire reign
of heaven, where the Most High welcomes people from
every nation. Jesus taught that the key commandments are to
love God and to love people. Christianity involves passing
this truth on to the next generation. God is so very near to
hearts devoted to loving, even when shown imperfectly. This
is a key worth sharing with your children's children.

Deuteronomy 4:1,5–9
Psalm 147:12–13,15–16,19–20
Matthew 5:17–19

Listen to my voice;
then I will be your God and you shall be
my people.
—JEREMIAH 7:23

It would be great if God had a unique ringtone that alerted our cell phones that the Almighty was calling. Imagine Jesus' picture popping up on the screen and having perfect reception when answering the call. His number would be saved in "favorites." God's ringtone also could get used when God called using someone else's number. How easy it would be to know to pay attention. It may appear to be a call from an old friend, but the ringtone announces that God is using this person to reach out. Be alert! It's one of God's people on the line, and God is speaking. Don't worry if you miss the call; God is persistent. If God leaves a voicemail, it's a message of acceptance and belonging.

Jeremiah 7:23–28
Psalm 95:1–2,6–7,8–9
Luke 11:14–23

Mary said, "Behold, I am the handmaid of the Lord.
May it be done to me according to your word."
—LUKE 1:38

Mary couldn't know fully what her yes meant. Over the next few months, her body would change in uncomfortable ways. Her womb would stretch as Christ grew within her. Having never experienced pregnancy before, she wouldn't know if her feelings were normal. We, too, are called to make room within for Christ, and sometimes the stretching is painful.

We don't know what saying yes to God will ultimately involve. It takes bravery to agree to a call. Life feels more certain, and in control, when we have a detailed plan. God doesn't provide those. God allows us to choose freely and to participate. Our capacity to hold and carry Christ grows as we allow ourselves to be stretched.

Isaiah 7:10–14; 8:10
Psalm 40:7–8a,8b–9,10,11
Hebrews 10:4–10
Luke 1:26–38

Saturday

MARCH 26

He will heal us;
he has struck us, but he will bind our wounds.
He will revive us after two days;
on the third day he will raise us up.
—HOSEA 6:1B

Eight centuries before Christ, Hosea's words hint at resurrection. Hardship and humiliation will precede it, but count on God: help is on the way. Hope for wellness and wholeness springs from a God who longs to demonstrate immense love. God reiterates a deep desire to be loved by humanity. How passionately and recklessly God loves. Some people do crazy things to show their love. They call countless times and send too many texts and emails. A familiar idiom states, "I'd go to the ends of the earth for you." God really does. Love revives, heals, and raises up new life.

Hosea 6:1–6
Psalm 51:3–4,18–19,20–21ab
Luke 18:9–14

The Pharisees and scribes began to complain.
—LUKE 15:2

Jesus responds to grousing Pharisees with the prodigal son
story. He sits to tell it, a sign of authority. People love
stories, so perhaps they leaned in, attentive. Jesus offers a
great buildup to the story's climax: the elder brother behaves
like the scribes and grumbles about the father's profligate
generosity. Jesus never tells whether this brother relents from
his complaining, nor does the writer tell how many of the
listeners relented either. Jesus leaves the story open-ended,
hoping hearts will be softened and converted. Was
Nicodemus in the crowd listening? What about Joseph of
Arimathea? They may have recognized themselves in the
older brother and, thanks to this story, turned toward a
genuine understanding of the love of God, so much deeper
than mere law.

Joshua 5:9a,10–12 or 1 Samuel 16:1b,6–7,10–13a
Psalm 34:2–3,4–5,6–7 (9a) or 23:1–3a,3b–4,5,6 (1)
2 Corinthians 5:17–21 or Ephesians 5:8–14
Luke 15:1–3,11–32 or John 9:1–41 or 9:1, 6–9, 13–17, 34–38

MARCH 28

Jesus said to him, "You may go; your son will live."
—JOHN 4:50

I imagine this man turning around immediately and excitedly rushing home, certain deep within that his gravely ill son would be well. He didn't even need to have Jesus join him. When have I had the kind of faith that acted on the strength of Scripture's teachings alone? How can I be the kind of disciple who trusts God so deeply that I know my loved ones and I will be rescued the minute I ask? As the psalmist says, "You did not let my enemies rejoice over me." God will never desert me, and that's a promise.

Isaiah 65:17–21 or Micah 7:7–9
Psalm 30:2 and 4,5–6,11–12a and 13b or 27:1, 7–8a, 8b–9abc, 13–14
John 4:43–54 or 9:1–41

Tuesday

MARCH 29

[Jesus said,] "Do you want to be well?"
—JOHN 5:6B

I had a surrogate grandfather whose parents died in the
Holocaust. He said, "The past is so compelling that I
sometimes find it very hard to live in the present." He was
weighed down by his escape and experiences during World
War II, and he suffered from depression. Sometimes I get
stuck, too. I offer God excuses while holding on to a past
hurt. I'd rather blame someone else for not "putting me into
the pool when the water is stirred up," or throw a pity party
in my suffering, or even put myself down for not stepping up.
Maybe I deny the pool is even there. God, grant me the
grace to dare look at my history from your point of view, that
I might accept the healing you want to give me.

Ezekiel 47:1–9,12
Psalm 46:2–3,5–6,8–9
John 5:1–16

Thus says the LORD:
In a time of favor I answer you,
on the day of salvation I help you;
And I have kept you.
—ISAIAH 49:8

These lines are dripping with love. Isaiah's poetic tenderness is consolation personified. Picture yourself lovingly enfolded in gently protective arms. God bends and kisses your forehead, dispelling all your fears and troubles. "I want to restore you," God says directly to you. Let yourself be freed. Never mind that you've been imprisoned. Come out and let yourself be seen by the God who favors you. Wait, you say, I cannot see this God. Like a mother who leaves her crying infant in a room alone while she runs to the kitchen to heat a bottle, God is already laboring to show favor to you. Be patient. The time of favor is coming.

Isaiah 49:8–15
Psalm 145:8–9,13cd–14,17–18
John 5:17–30

Thursday

MARCH 31

[Moses said,] "Let your blazing wrath die down;
relent in punishing your people."
—EXODUS 32:12B

Not again! thinks Moses. "Those people frustrate me beyond
belief! Now what are those calf builders doing? God! I beg you;
I implore you, don't give my people and my children what they
deserve for abandoning you. Of course, they're mistaken and
will get only grief from prioritizing gold as a god. It will be
empty for them. Forgive them for imitating the practices of
nations around us! They don't really know what they're doing.
What? You *will* forgive them again? You really took my request
to heart? Wow. Thank you. You really are incredible, God. If I
were you, I would've carried out my threats of punishment. You
are so not like me. And I am truly grateful."

Exodus 32:7–14
Psalm 106:19–20,21–22,23
John 5:31–47

*With revilement and torture let us put him to the test that we may have
proof of his gentleness and try his patience.*
—WISDOM 2:19

Think about a time when you felt tested. Perhaps it was
disheartening news or a job loss. What did you learn, or did
some virtue or resilience grow within you? How did this
testing strengthen your ability to show compassion to others
who struggle? Jesus' disciples can expect to encounter trials
and even ridicule. It takes courage to remain at peace amidst
difficulties. And virtues grow the more they are tested. It may
seem like a terrible system, but we can't know what God has in
mind. Imagine what you would say to someone else being
crushed by adversity. Your experience can help someone else's
faith, so that they can endure this test, and the one after that.

Wisdom 2:1a, 12–22
Psalm 34:17–18,19–20,21 and 23
John 7:1–2, 10, 25–30

Saturday

APRIL 2

• ST. FRANCIS OF PAOLA, HERMIT •

"Does our law condemn a man before it first
hears him
and finds out what he is doing?"
—JOHN 7:51

I assume that the shabbily dressed man wants a handout, so I avert my eyes as I pass. "Do you want me to pray with you?" he asks. Did I hear him right? I stop and turn. "You look upset," he says, "Can I pray for you?" Prejudgment leads to seeing what I expect to see. How often do I judge someone by their clothes, by the way they're treating their child while shopping, or by some other external characteristic that obscures the likeness of God within? In today's Gospel, the guards witnessed someone speaking as they'd never heard before. Something authentic was shining in Jesus. Returning to people who hadn't seen what they had, the guards struggled to explain themselves. Those who prejudged couldn't understand.

Jeremiah 11:18–20
Psalm 7:2–3,9bc–10,11–12
John 7:40–53

Forgetting what lies behind
but straining forward to what lies ahead,
I continue my pursuit toward the goal,
the prize of God's upward calling, in Christ Jesus.
—PHILIPPIANS 3:13–14

Picture a well-trained runner, dressed and ready. She's got her toe on the starting block, and all her mental focus is on how to reach the finish. Distractions tempt her, but she competes to win. A blast sounds. The runners are off! A crowd of witnesses in heaven cheers and inspires the contestant. She drives her body on. In the stands is St. Paul, who's closely following the race. It's a marathon, not a sprint. Eternal life may be around the next lap. Past mistakes, pulled muscles, and long workouts were worth it. The runner is fully present to the moment, aware that the prize at the end is eternal life with Jesus.

Isaiah 43:16–21 or Ezekiel 37:12–14
Psalm 126:1–2,2–3,4–5,6 (3) or 130:1–2,3–4,5–6,7–8
Philippians 3:8–14 or Romans 8:8–11
John 11:1–45 or 11:3–7, 17, 20–27, 33b–45

*You spread the table before me
in the sight of my foes;
You anoint my head with oil;
my cup overflows.*
—PSALM 23:5

These words praise God by describing how the Almighty does great things for humanity. They also sound indirectly like gratitude. The mnemonic ACTS serves as a reminder of the various types of prayer: adoration, contrition, thanksgiving, and supplication. Some people pray most frequently in supplication, interceding for others or offering God a list of requests. Imagine Susanna in the sight of her foes, crying to God for relief from her enemies. And God delivered. Be confident in God's protecting deliverance as well, which will lead to praise and thanksgiving.

Daniel 13:1–9,15–17,19–30,33–62 or 13:41c–62 or 2 Kings 4:18b–21,32–37
Psalm 23:1–3a,3b–4,5,6 or 17:1,6–7,8b and 15 or 17:1, 6–7, 8b and 15
John 8:12–20 or 11:1–45

Tuesday

APRIL 5

• ST. VINCENT FERRER, PRIEST •

Incline your ear to me;
in the day when I call, answer me speedily.
—PSALM 102:3

The small faith community always begins with checking in about how God has been at work since they last met. The five people who meet weekly pray in silence first, reminding themselves that Jesus is present. After the allotted time passes on this particular day, a woman shyly says, "I got a message!"

The others eagerly wait as she overcomes her embarrassment. After a pause, she says in a subdued voice, "I was crucified; you will get through this difficult time." Everyone breathes. A second participant now admits to feeling Jesus saying something personal: "Stop being so judgmental. Relax. See Jesus in everyone." The group members nod in silent reverence, recognizing that God truly speaks to human hearts in our day.

Numbers 21:4–9
Psalm 102:2–3,16–18,19–21
John 8:21–30

⇒ 129 ⇐

Wednesday
APRIL 6

• OPTIONAL MASS FOR FIFTH WEEK IN LENT •

When Martha heard that Jesus was coming,
she went to meet him.
—JOHN 11:20

Martha wasn't one to sit around, whether that meant trying
to get Jesus' help in making her sister work in the kitchen or
running to the dusty road when Lazarus died and her good
Friend was arriving. She was a woman of action. "Oh, Jesus,"
Martha laments as she falls into his brotherly arms. "What
took you so long?" She was the kind of friend who could say
that to him. As this passage says, they loved each other. Her
relationship with Jesus meant she felt safe telling him exactly
what she experienced, even when overwrought, needlessly
upset, or faltering in faith. What a great example. Make time
daily to run out to meet Jesus when you sense that he's
approaching.

2 Kings 4:18b–21,32–37
Psalm 17:1,6–7,8b, and 15
John 11:1–45

So they picked up stones to throw at him;
but Jesus hid and went out of the temple area.
—JOHN 8:59

Jesus tried to convince those in the temple not only that he
was *from* God but also that God was his father. But his
listeners, some of whom had witnessed his miracles, refused
to accept his message. Jesus as God could have created
undeniable proof to convince them, but no. His humanity
was important, too. As St. Ignatius puts it, divinity hides
itself at times in Jesus, especially on the cross. Jesus hid from
stones; did it involve divine power to evade them? Jesus
exercised his freedom to preach, to push the status quo, and
to lead to Abba. God guides us to greater detachment, but
that doesn't eliminate discord and angry opposition. Follow
Jesus? Expect rejection.

Genesis 17:3–9
Psalm 105:4–5,6–7,8–9
John 8:51–59

Friday
APRIL 8

*All those who were my friends
are on the watch for any misstep of mine.*
—JEREMIAH 20:10B

Good Friday is next week. Lent is mostly behind you now,
and how did your resolutions fare? Have you fasted as you
hoped to, given more generously to the needy, served in new
ways, and prayed more? You may be your own worst critic,
able to notice every failure you make. If the season you
experienced felt short of transformative, that's okay. Small
steps add up. You never know what people watching you
might glean from your efforts. God can do something great,
even with missteps. God is still working in you, and you can
sing praise to God who rescues you, even from yourself.

Jeremiah 20:10–13
Psalm 18:2–3a,3bc–4,5–6,7
John 10:31–42

Jesus no longer walked about in public
among the Jews
but he left for the region near the desert.
—JOHN 11:54

Two years ago on this night, I was practicing to lector for
Palm Sunday using a Zoom meeting. About eight people
sheltering in place signed in online. It was new for most of
us. Because of the coronavirus pandemic, we were preparing
for a Holy Week like none before. With no procession, my
husband and I would simply sit in our dining room and tune
in. On this night, we tested our home's lighting and sound. I
revised a distracting background by forming a cross from
palms gathered on a solitary neighborhood walk. It was a
somber time—a desert experience. Deprived of being
together, we wanted to gather as one assembly all the more.
Oh, were we hungry for Eucharist!

Ezekiel 37:21–28
Jeremiah 31:10,11–12abcd,13
John 11:45–56

Sunday

APRIL 10

• PALM SUNDAY OF THE PASSION OF THE LORD •

*Christ Jesus, though he was in the form of God,
did not regard equality with God
something to be grasped.*
—PHILIPPIANS 2:6

What about me? Hey. Notice me. Hello? What about my concerns, my place in line, my needs? I want to be the one in charge. These attitudes are the opposite of the Messiah's. Jesus is completely emptying himself for us. He turns over control of his very body to torturers. He doesn't put his own financial security, personal comfort, or even his basic human needs ahead of the Father's will. The life of Jesus is radical. As we enter this holiest of the year's weeks, let's look at how we strive to be godlike. Let us repent once again.

PROCESSION:
Luke 19:28–40

MASS:
Isaiah 50:4–7
Psalm 22:8–9,17–18,19–20,23–24 (2a)
Philippians 2:6–11
Luke 22:14—23:56

The house was filled with the fragrance of the oil.
—JOHN 12:3B

Noses are critical to memory. Baking bread reminds me of college and coming home to my grandmother pulling loaves from the oven. The whole house felt cozy. I sniff bread now and see my grandmother in a flower-print apron, leaning over her dough. What associations did Lazarus's family have as weeks later their home still bore the aroma of that costly nard? It likely dripped from Jesus' feet onto the floor or into a foot-washing basin. And Mary's hair surely absorbed it. Did that scent always instill glee as they remembered their first experience of the resurrected One in their home? This anointing took place six days before the Messiah's final earthly Passover. Did Martha, who this reading says was doing her usual thing—serving—always associate that aroma with her love for Jesus?

Isaiah 42:1–7
Psalm 27:1,2,3,13–14
John 12:1–11

Tuesday

APRIL 12

• TUESDAY OF HOLY WEEK •

Jesus answered him,
"Where I am going, you cannot follow me now,
though you will follow later."
—JOHN 13:36

If the readings yesterday, today, and tomorrow sound familiar, that's because every year, regardless of the cycle, the church uses these specific passages. It offers opportunities to commit the verses to memory. Here, Jesus is at his last supper, and he's heavyhearted. What's interesting about today's reading is that it leaves out verses 34 and 35, which are words everyone ought to have memorized: "I give you a new commandment: love one another. As I have loved you, so you also should love one another. This is how all will know that you are my disciples, if you have love for one another." These words are like a golden nugget of what it means to follow Christ.

Isaiah 49:1–6
Psalm 71:1–2,3–4a,5ab–6ab,15 and 17
John 13:21–33,36–38

*The Lord GOD has given me
a well-trained tongue,
That I might know how to speak to the weary
a word that will rouse them.*

—ISAIAH 50:4

This reading describes every follower of Jesus, even quiet ones. Baptized priest, prophet, and royalty, every Christian is gifted to be all three, whether it's evident to the believer or not. God intends each person to offer encouraging, uplifting words and actions so that others are urged toward goodness and love. To do this is to be prophetic. Someone in your life needs to hear a message only you can deliver, but what is it, and who needs to hear it? Pick one area in which to be prophetic, to tell it like it is, with love and a desire to inspire. Speak intentional words that assist someone who is weary. Support someone whose spiritual health is wavering.

Isaiah 50:4–9a
Psalm 69:8–10,21–22,31 and 33–34
Matthew 26:14–25

Thursday
APRIL 14

• THURSDAY OF HOLY WEEK (HOLY THURSDAY) •

[God said,] "This day shall be a memorial feast for you,
which all your generations shall celebrate."
—EXODUS 12:14

Contemplate Our Lady's thoughts: When the youngest child
recited, "Why is tonight different from every other night?" I
felt that this Passover *was* different. I could sense it in my Son.
The mood at supper was different; when he left for the Garden
of Gethsemane, I felt a heaviness. I wanted to go with them.
But no, my place was with the women. They worked to clean
up after the enormous meal. Imagine the dishes from thirteen
men, friends, and many family members! It's good we rented a
large room. I watched my son from the doorway for a long
time. Why do I feel different from every other night, watching
my Son? I will pray and await his return.

CHRISM MASS:
Isaiah 61:1–3a,6a,8b–9
Psalm 89:21–22,25 and 27
Revelation 1:5–8
Luke 4:16–21

EVENING MASS OF THE
LORD'S SUPPER:
Exodus 12:1–8,11–14
Psalm 116:12–13,15–16bc,17–18
1 Corinthians 11:23–26
John 13:1–15

Friday

APRIL 15

• FRIDAY OF THE PASSION OF THE LORD (GOOD FRIDAY) •

We had all gone astray like sheep,
each following his own way;
but the LORD laid upon him
the guilt of us all.
—ISAIAH 53:6

Lost in the brambles, the sheep bleats for rescue. It cannot extract itself from its debilitating situation. It needs a savior. It's going to hurt the rescuer to join the sheep among the thorns. The shepherd will be scraped and wounded after liberating the sheep. He will need to get down and join the sheep in its trapped place in the brambles. The sheep cries, "Baa! Ab-baa! Abba!" The enormity of Jesus' steps to the cross is incomprehensible.

Isaiah 52:13—53:12
Psalm 31:2,6,12–13,15–16,17,25
Hebrews 4:14–16; 5:7–9
John 18:1—19:42

Saturday
APRIL 16

• HOLY SATURDAY •

The Egyptians sounded the retreat before Israel,
because the LORD was fighting for them.
—EXODUS 14:25B

This is the night when God led Israel's children from slavery in Egypt and made them pass dry-shod through the Red Sea. This is the night on which God with a pillar of fire banished the darkness of sin. This is the night throughout the world that even now sets Christian believers apart from worldly vices and from the gloom of sin. Then and now, God labors for the people. Christ's triumph comes when circumstances appear dire. The light of Christ overcomes evil. It's not accomplished by God's people on their own.

VIGIL:
Genesis 1:1—2:2 or 1:1,26–31a
Psalm 104:1–2,5–6,10,12,13–14,24,35 or
33:4–5,6–7,12–13,20 and 22 (5b)
Genesis 22:1–18 or 22:1–2,9a,10–13,15–18
Psalm 16:5,8,9–10,11
Exodus 14:15—15:1
Exodus 15:1–2,3–4,5–6,17–18 (1b)
Isaiah 54:5–14
Psalm 30:2,4,5–6,11–12,13 (2a)
Isaiah 55:1–11
Isaiah 12:2–3,4,5–6

Baruch 3:9–15,32—4:4
Psalm 19:8,9,10,11
Ezekiel 36:16–17a,18–28
Psalm 42:3,5; 43:3,4 or Isaiah
12:2–3,4bcd,5–6 (3) or Psalm
51:12–13,14–15,18–19
Romans 6:3–11
Psalm 118:1–2,16–17,22–23
Luke 24:1–12

Sunday

APRIL 17

• EASTER SUNDAY OF THE RESURRECTION OF THE LORD •

He is not here, but he has been raised.
—LUKE 24:6

Families in a church in Illinois made a joy-filled video using Handel's "Hallelujah Chorus," written in 1741. In fast clips in time with the music, children jump out from behind trees, each holding a sign with a syllable of *hallelujah*. Others tell the Good News by standing on porches, patios, rooftops, and trampolines. One family sequentially pulls syllables, written on plates, out of their dishwasher. Hilarious and fun. You can't help smiling. Viral videos are a metaphor for Easter itself. The good news of Jesus spans time and place. Generations raise hallelujahs. Love and salvation fire up countless hearts. It's time for that let-it-all-out joy of Easter. He's alive!

Acts 10:34a,37–43
Psalm 118:1–2,16–17,22–23
Colossians 3:1–4 or 1 Corinthians 5:6b–8
John 20:1–9 or Lk 24:1–12 or, at an afternoon or evening Mass, Luke 24:13–35

Monday

APRIL 18

You will show me the path to life,
fullness of joys in your presence,
the delights at your right hand forever.
—PSALM 16:11

What does the path of life look like today? Early this
morning, it was a freeway as I drove to a doctor's
appointment. Later it was a broken sidewalk where it would
be easy to trip. Then I bicycled across bumpy asphalt streets
to get to a one o'clock meeting. The path of my fingers on
the phone, computer, and paperwork was busy today.
Hunger drew my feet to the kitchen. God, you were there
every step of the journey. You were guiding my path even
when I wasn't noticing, and I feel joy knowing that you were
always at my side.

Acts 2:14,22–33
Psalm 16:1–2a and 5,7–8,9–10,11
Matthew 28:8–15

Tuesday

APRIL 19

Mary went and announced to the disciples,
"I have seen the Lord,"
and then reported what he had told her.
—JOHN 20:18

I bubbled with the exciting news: another grandchild was on the way. The joy ran through me all day like persistent music. I couldn't wait to tell everyone. I wonder if Mary felt like this. I imagine she ran excitedly from grave to upper room. She may have passed acquaintances on the way, wishing she could tell them. But no, Jesus sent her to the disciples, and they would be the first to hear. She glowed with unquenchable joy. Jesus was risen. It all made sense now. They would see it, too, she was sure of it. She would announce the Resurrection based on her experience with Jesus, who gave her a mission: preach.

Acts 2:36–41
Psalm 33:4–5,18–19,20 and 22
John 20:11–18

Wednesday
APRIL 20

*They said to each other,
"Were not our hearts burning within us
while he spoke to us on the way and opened
the Scriptures to us?"*
—LUKE 24:32

Wouldn't you love for Jesus to walk with you for two hours, explaining Scripture? In your present circumstances, how do you know when God is communicating with you? God surely relates to each person, but learning God's language can be difficult. Some people describe hearing God—their experience of a burning within—as "It happened in a flash" or "I came to understand" or "From somewhere 'not me' I had a sense. I didn't hear words exactly, but I clearly knew." You can bet the couple returning from Emmaus talked all night with the apostles, excitedly exchanging stories and insights. "I never thought about it that way before . . ."

Acts 3:1–10
Psalm 105:1–2,3–4,6–7,8–9
Luke 24:13–35

Thursday

APRIL 21

• THURSDAY WITHIN THE OCTAVE OF EASTER •

You are the children of the prophets
and of the covenant that God made
with your ancestors.
—ACTS 3:25

For a small fee you can have your DNA studied, and you'll discover your biological ancestry. No such tests exist for your ancestry of faith. You learned about Jesus Christ from someone, who learned from someone, who learned from someone, and on and on all the way back some two thousand years. Do you ever think about the ancestry of your faith? From which strain did your belief system originally grow? Perhaps it was Thomas, who evangelized in India. Possibly it was descendants of Lazarus in Greece. Take a moment to thank God for the many ancestors of your faith. It's quite a family.

Acts 3:11–26
Psalm 8:2ab and 5,6–7,8–9
Luke 24:35–48

Jesus said to them, "Come, have breakfast."
—JOHN 21:12

Fish never tasted so good, Peter probably thought as he ate the fresh catch cooked on a fire by Jesus, his friend. Meals often taste better when you're with people you love. Think about how you eat, whether you savor each bite or mindlessly hurry, looking down at an empty plate and wondering where the food went. See if you can really enjoy each bite the next time you have breakfast. Change a habit over your eating, whether it be adding a short prayer of gratitude at the end or building some silent appreciation into the meal. Jesus invites you today to an intimate repast. And the next time you approach Eucharist, remember the invitation: "Come. Have breakfast with Me."

Acts 4:1–12
Psalm 118:1–2 and 4,22–24,25–27a
John 21:1–14

I shall not die, but live
and declare the works of the LORD.
—PSALM 118:17

Every living thing dies. It's inevitable. But thanks to Jesus, things don't end there. As signs of spring emerge, all of creation bursts with a silent song of joy. Yes, death is inevitable, but resurrection is real. Jesus orders us to get out and tell the good news that we were made to live forever with God, that God is ever ready to forgive sins, and that we're loved by God with an inconceivable love. Alleluia!

Acts 4:13–21
Psalm 118:1 and 14–15ab,16–18,19–21
Mark 16:9–15

Sunday

APRIL 24

Now Jesus did many other signs in the presence
of his disciples
that are not written in this book.
—JOHN 20:31

The whole world could not contain all the volumes that could be published if every sign Jesus ever worked were to be written down. Each life is full of signs, miracles, and oft-forgotten or taken-for-granted experiences that are divine encounters. God is subtle and is quietly laboring all the time for people, through people. Why not keep a journal of some of every day's minimiracles? We all have them; we don't always know that we do. A breakthrough with a family member may not be a coincidence; it's a God-incident.

Acts 5:12–16
Psalm 118:2–4,13–15,22–24
Revelation 1:9–11a,12–13,17–19
John 20:19–31

Cast all your worries upon him because he cares for you.
Be sober and vigilant.
—1 PETER 5:7–8A

A fisherman lets the bait fly. Off it goes! It's on its own. Or is it?
Soon it's back in the fisherman's grasp, only now it's stuck in a
hungry, gasping fish. Trusting God and paying attention sound
simple, but casting off worry with no strings attached is tough.
How can someone really worry about nothing? It's just human
nature to fret, right? Think about how to be vigilant for ways
that worry sneaks up and insidiously tries to find a foothold.
God is in all things and all around, but other influences are also
at play. Be ready, keeping vision alert, and don't let God pass
by without noticing. Don't get hooked by worry.

1 Peter 5:5b–14
Psalm 89:2–3,6–7,16–17
Mark 16:15–20

Tuesday

APRIL 26

*With great power the Apostles bore witness
to the resurrection of the Lord Jesus,
and great favor was accorded them all.*
—ACTS 4:33

I remember teaching a class of third graders who had never
experienced any religious instruction. One day I let it
casually drop that Jesus got up from the dead. One boy
interrupted. "Wait. What? You mean he got up from the
dead?" Yes, I assured him, surprised that he knew that Jesus
was crucified but didn't know that Jesus came back to life! I
was privileged to bear witness to the Resurrection and see
amazement cross a boy's face. He helped me see that our
world still has people in it who don't realize that the
resurrection of Jesus happened. I was sure his parents knew,
but they needed help teaching their child. Who else needs
help fully comprehending the saving love of the risen One?

Acts 4:32–37
Psalm 93:1ab,1cd–2,5
John 3:7b–15

Wednesday
APRIL 27

When the poor one called out, the LORD heard,
and from all his distress [God] saved him.
—PSALM 34:7

Sometimes the Lord hears the poor by sending us. Of course, we have the freedom to say no to God's request that we go. Whenever we respond affirmatively to the Almighty, God deserves the credit for any alleviation of distress that we accomplish. We stand in the place of God by listening, holding a hand, and offering the body language that says we care. We lean in, and God is present where two or three gather in difficult times. And when we are the poor ones, we can search for God in our brothers and sisters for God's response to our plea. God always answers. And God hears through us.

Acts 5:17–26
Psalm 34:2–3,4–5,6–7,8–9
John 3:16–21

Thursday

APRIL 28

He does not ration his gift of the Spirit.
—JOHN 3:34

How limited we human beings are! We have only so much patience, so much willingness to forgive, and only so much energy after a long day. Do we impose small expectations on God? We don't ask for the Holy Spirit's gifts in measures that God is willing to pour out. If the disciples, thanks to the Holy Spirit, stood courageous before the Sanhedrin and continued to preach and heal, why don't we ask for an abundant outpouring of the same Holy Spirit on our day? Our low expectations limit what God can provide. But God is eager to lavish grace upon us. The Easter season is the perfect time to ask for an extra portion of the gifts of the Holy Spirit.

Acts 5:27–33
Psalm 34:2 and 9,17–18,19–20
John 3:31–36

Friday

APRIL 29

• ST. CATHERINE OF SIENA, VIRGIN AND DOCTOR OF THE CHURCH •

Wait for the LORD with courage;
be stouthearted, and wait for the LORD.
—PSALM 27:14

The evening news report discouraged me again that night. I knew I needed more courage to do something about it because I was tempted to despair. God, why do you allow this!? For the moment, I needed to escape, to pray, and to wait. My husband switched the channel to something calming. Within minutes, technology filled our home with sounds of peaceful ocean waves. And I recalled the words of St. Catherine of Siena: "God, you are an ocean of mercy. You are a clear sea full of sweet secrets." I returned to a balanced attitude. Yes, I could relax into God's buoying presence and let go of fear. My devoted Abba, who holds all in a loving embrace, could grant me the grace to be brave.

Acts 5:34–42
Psalm 27:1,4,13–14
John 6:1–15

Saturday

APRIL 30

• ST. PIUS V, POPE •

Give thanks to the LORD on the harp;
with the ten-stringed lyre chant his praises.
—PSALM 33:2

The person who sings, prays twice, according to St. Augustine. I'm one of those people whose primary prayer style involves music. I don't play a harp, but recorded music puts a symphony of instruments into my headset. Listening to Christian music in the background gives me a sense that somewhere inside me, I am kneeling in the presence of the Most High, even though outwardly I'm working, typing, exercising, shopping, or doing something else. Do you know which style of prayer is the best way for you to feel God present and laboring alongside you?

Acts 6:1–7
Psalm 33:1–2,4–5,18–19
John 6:16–21

At that time, Jesus revealed himself again to his disciples at the Sea of Tiberias.

—JOHN 21:1

If you were Jesus, would you be appearing to your friends in the ways Scripture records? Would you pop in front of them in an upper room, scaring them into thinking you were a ghost? Would you be casually walking alongside, like on the road to Emmaus, waiting to be noticed? Would you be sitting on a beach cooking fish? Jesus is still mysterious, surprising, and awe-inspiring. How do you expect Jesus to appear to you? If you've met him in the disguise of a poor person, did you dare ask if she was the Lord, or did you just share breakfast? The truth is, *you* are Jesus to people all around you. Anytime you manifest love, Christ is in your midst (Matthew 18:20).

Acts 5:27–32,40b–41
Psalm 30:2,4,5–6,11–12,13 (2a)
Revelation 5:11–14
John 21:1–19 or 21:1–14

• ST. ATHANASIUS, BISHOP AND DOCTOR OF THE CHURCH •

Do not work for food that perishes
but for the food that endures for eternal life,
which the Son of Man will give you.
—JOHN 6:27

Notice how Jesus uses a physical human-survival need to
point out humanity's ability to starve spiritually without God.
When it comes to the soul's hierarchy of needs, time with
God is as important as food and water are to the body. When
the basic needs are met, people can turn to other pursuits.
From prayer grows service. In the first reading, Stephen's
preaching gives him imperishable sustenance, evidenced in
his face glowing like an angel's. He is about to review
salvation history for Jewish leaders, culminating in their poor
treatment of Jesus. It's a dramatic scene. In the field of souls,
the paychecks are out of this world.

Acts 6:8–15
Psalm 119:23–24,26–27,29–30
John 6:22–29

Tuesday

MAY 3

• ST. PHILIP AND ST. JAMES, APOSTLES •

"If you ask anything of me in my name, I will do it."
—JOHN 14:14

How might Philip have responded to Jesus? Did he dare to be completely honest? "Teacher, forgive me for still needing clarification. We're close friends, so I feel I can ask you anything. And this may sound like a dumb question—James, I see you snickering over there—Jesus, what do you mean that we can ask you for anything and you'll do it? Anything? Is this another parable? I honestly am not sure what you will and won't do. You are in the Father, and the Father is in you, and we are in you, and so we are in the Father? Help me, Jesus. I still don't understand. I'm afraid I'll need some special gift to figure this out. I'm still in a fog."

1 Corinthians 15:1–8
Psalm 19:2–3,4–5
John 14:6–14

Wednesday

MAY 4

"For this is the will of my Father,
that everyone who sees the Son and believes in him
may have eternal life."
—JOHN 6:40

We get to go to heaven, and a place is waiting there for each
of us. It's better than a surprise party, free tickets to our
favorite sporting event, and winning a lottery combined.
This is cause for rejoicing, and now is the time of year to sing
with gusto some extra *alleluias* in the middle of an ordinary
day. Can God ever get enough alleluias? The priest ends
Mass with a special "Go in peace, alleluia, alleluia!" and we
sing back, "Thanks be to God! Alleluia, alleluia!" The
Resurrection is such a big deal that we ought to go overboard
with praise.

Acts 8:1b–8
Psalm 66:1–3a,4–5,6–7a
John 6:35–40

Thursday

MAY 5

"I am the living bread that came down from heaven;
whoever eats this bread will live forever."
—JOHN 6:51

Christ's listeners are complaining again. Jesus can see it on
their faces as they mumble-grumble to each other. "Look,"
Jesus says flat out. "God my Abba sent me, and I'm the one
who will be raising you on the last day." As Jesus seems to
talk in circles about people listening to the Father who points
to Jesus and Jesus following the Father, his audience will soon
have more to murmur about. Eucharist is the real flesh of
Christ. Jesus makes no exceptions when he teaches that he is
the living bread, and they must ingest him. His blood,
poured out, runs in our veins. This was no parable or
metaphor. Jews fought among themselves. Some left. Jesus
stood his ground. Will you?

Acts 8:26–40
Psalm 66:8–9,16–17,20
John 6:44–51

> [Ananias said,] *"Saul, my brother, the Lord has sent me,*
> *Jesus who appeared to you on the way."*
> —ACTS 9:17

God, did I hear you right? Is this really you, or is it all in my head? You want me to get up *now*? And go to Straight Street to seek out Saul? This guy is trying to imprison people like me. What am I going to tell my wife? If I do this, I may suffer greatly. Why would you choose Saul—a man who is blind in more ways than one—as your instrument? Okay. I know this is an authentic, extraordinary divine request. I always say that I'd do anything for you. I'll go. I'm ashamed to admit that I feel better knowing you will allow him to suffer for Jesus' name. I don't have to judge or punish him. You only ask me to love.

Acts 9:1–20
Psalm 117:1bc,2
John 6:52–59

Saturday

MAY 7

*I will offer a sacrifice of praise
and call on the name of the LORD*
—PSALM 116:17

When you make daily gratitude lists, your appreciation of
little things grows. Thankfulness breeds more thankfulness,
and that leads to praise. Try a popcorn prayer with others:
everyone names something they're grateful for, without
taking turns. People just say reasons they want to thank and
praise God (for life! roses! notebooks! books! sleep! pillows!),
and when it overlaps with someone else, it's just like popcorn
bursting in erratic blasts. Allow your thanksgiving to pop out
wildly! Savor gratitude, like butter on the tip of your tongue.
End with three *alleluias*. It's the Easter season, after all. Don't
forget to express joyful praise that Jesus is alive!

Acts 9:31–42
Psalm 116:12–13,14–15,16–17
John 6:60–69

Sunday

MAY 8

• FOURTH SUNDAY OF EASTER •

And God will wipe away every tear from their eyes.
—REVELATION 7:17B

Some of the reasons for tears, St. Catherine of Siena
explained, are sorrow, healing, pain, regret, and
overwhelming joy. Tears can be unleashed by strong love.
Tears are a gift. They cleanse the soul. Parents see a child's
tears with empathy and compassion, sometimes shedding
tears of their own. Taking up one's cross means loving others
through their tears, too. God's presence is at work in the lives
of those who weep. Followers of Jesus walk alongside those
who cry. God invites all people to wipe away tears as in
imitation of the Beloved, Jesus. St. Catherine calls these
unitive tears, where the two are joined. "Such a soul receives
the fruit of spiritual calm, an emotional union with my gentle
divine nature" (*The Dialogue*, 96).

Acts 13:14,43–52
Psalm 100:1–2,3,5
Revelation 7:9,14b–17
John 10:27–30

Monday

MAY 9

[Jesus said,] "I am the gate.
Whoever enters through me will be saved."
—JOHN 10:9

The loudspeaker blares: "Now boarding flight 2301 to heaven at gate B16. All ticketed passengers proceed to the gate. Ten minutes before departure, the gate will be closed." I think I have all the time in the world, but when is my flight for the reign of God taking off? I have only this moment guaranteed. Will I be allowed through the security gate, or will I have liquids and gels and sins exceeding the limits? People line up, but no one gets down that Jetway without a scan and a nod through the gate. Jesus, you are my gate and airbridge from the terminal. I feel secure knowing it's going to be a safe journey and an exciting ride. My hoped-for destination will be perfect.

Acts 11:1–18
Psalm 42:2–3; 43:3,4
John 10:1–10

Tuesday

MAY 10

• ST. DAMIEN DE VEUSTER, PRIEST •

[The Jews said to him,] "If you are the Christ, tell us plainly."
Jesus answered them, "I told you and you do not believe me."
—JOHN 10:24–25

It's easy for me to chide the Jews for not believing Jesus, who stood right there. But how many times have I disbelieved God's unshakable love for me? I think, *Could God really forget about that infraction of mine?* Then there's me not trusting God with every decision or even with my day. The world seems to be in another unsolvable mess, despite the song that he's got the whole thing in his hands. Oh dear. God, forgive my unbelief again. You love me; you are *the* Way, the embodiment of Truth, and Light in darkness. Help me when my faith fails.

Acts 11:19–26
Psalm 87:1b–3,4–5,6–7
John 10:22–30

Wednesday
MAY 11

[Jesus said,] "I did not come to condemn the world but to save the world.
—JOHN 12:47

Why are so many people eager to judge, criticize, and call out mistakes? The world is full of people rejoicing in someone's fall. Jesus didn't become human to point a finger at people or to induce shame. Why do we do those things to one another? Jesus promoted forgiving countless times and showing mercy. God so loved the world that the Son came to redeem it, not destroy it with divisions. Jesus wanted us all to be one, just as he and the Father are. How can we do a better job of overlooking offenses? St. Ignatius of Loyola advised people to put a good interpretation on a neighbor's statement rather than condemn it. Always assume the best.

Acts 12:24—13:5a
Psalm 67:2–3,5,6 and 8
John 12:44–50

Thursday

MAY 12

[The synagogue officials said,] "My brothers, if one of you has a word of exhortation
for the people, please speak."
—ACTS 13:15

Words are powerful. They can cut or encourage, deflate or uplift. My grandson said he was sad because his brother said something hurtful. I comforted him, saying, "I had three brothers. I understand." Every day I have opportunities to offer a word of consolation to someone. "Come on! You can do it!" It can be done via social media even. God calls me to speak joy, solidarity, compassion, and love. How can I better pay attention to my words today? Will I, like St. Paul and his friends, be given an opportunity to speak truth to some audience? Will those listening react with skepticism, criticism, or conversion? I can't know. I should speak it anyway. Dare to be humiliated. All the best people are.

Acts 13:13–25
Psalm 89:2–3,21–22,25 and 27
John 13:16–20

Friday

MAY 13

• OUR LADY OF FATIMA •

Serve the LORD with fear, and rejoice before him;
with trembling rejoice.
—PSALM 2:11

In October 1917, a large crowd witnessed the sun trembling over a field north of Lisbon. People put away their umbrellas and fell to their knees. Extraordinary solar movement convinced many that their faith in God was well-founded. Consciences were stung with remorse and people rededicated themselves to prayer. The Mother of God invited people to move closer to her Son. Three humble, quivering children had told authorities boldly about visions of the Lady with the rosary. The children stood by their convictions. Mary's messages beckoned people to penance, prayer, and conversion. It was a serious exhortation to rejoice in God the Savior, who does mighty things for us. The invitation was to respond with generosity.

Acts 13:26–33
Psalm 2:6–7,8–9,10–11ab
John 14:1–6

Saturday

MAY 14

• ST. MATTHIAS, APOSTLE •

They prayed, "You, Lord, who know the hearts of all,
show which one of these two you have chosen
to take the place in this apostolic ministry."

—ACTS 1:24

God can use anything to communicate with us, even dice. When faith is strong, God's voice beckons through some pretty amazing avenues. Matthias won the lottery. Imagine the faith of the eleven apostles who felt compelled to be twelve again. Was the mood solemn or celebratory? What other discernment steps narrowed the field down to two? Matthias moved from being just one of many followers of Jesus to becoming an important leader. And what became of the other guy? Imagine them both humbly rooting for the other to be selected. When the Jesuits select a new superior general, they never choose anyone who's vying for it. St. Ignatius never wanted the job. Did Matthias feel that way?

Acts 1:15–17,20–26
Psalm 113:1–2,3–4,5–6,7–8
John 15:9–17

Sunday

MAY 15

• FIFTH SUNDAY OF EASTER •

*[I heard,] "Behold, God's dwelling is with the human race.
He will dwell with them and they will be his people
and God himself will always be with them as their God."*
—REVELATION 21:3

Think about it: you are God's very own house. Even if you
see your inner room as a broom closet, Jesus wants to hang
out there. Maybe he picks up a broom and starts sweeping.
Let's imagine that you dare to open your inner room, but
when you peek in, it's a mess. Quickly you slam the door.
Jesus stands before you and says, "Let's go in together." When
you reopen the door, the room is spotless. Jesus removed all
traces of sin. You enter peacefully an inner castle, as St.
Teresa of Ávila described the heart. Christ in Eucharist is
inside your body. Adore the One who lives within.

Acts 14:21–27
Psalm 145:8–9,10–11,12–13 (see 1)
Revelation 21:1–5a
John 13:31–33a,34–35

Monday

MAY 16

[Jesus said,] "The advocate, the Holy Spirit
whom the Father will send in my name—
he will teach you everything
and remind you of all that I told you."
—JOHN 14:26

List making. Reminders on phones, email notifications, and calendars. What prompts you to remember important things? The Holy Spirit is with you to remind you of everything that Jesus taught while he walked the earth; the list includes *Love each other. Forgive without limit. Bless others with service. Be honest.*

But how do you remind yourself to pay attention to the Spirit? The *examen* prayer works more effectively than an alarm on a phone. Ask for light, invite the Holy Spirit in, and review the day as the Spirit sees it. Repent as needed, and look ahead, knowing that the Spirit, sent in Jesus' name, will be present.

Acts 14:5–18
Psalm 115:1–2,3–4,15–16
John 14:21–26

Tuesday

MAY 17

Let all your works give you thanks, O LORD,
and let your faithful ones bless you.
—PSALM 145:10

Many plants have life spans much longer than ours. They were praising God by being rooted in that soil long before we were born. The oldest known plant on earth—3,266 years old—is in California in Giant Sequoia National Monument. Isn't that amazing? People standing at the foot of a giant sequoia tree feel tiny. One tree weighs close to three million pounds. How do we gain perspective trying to comprehend its immensity? God chuckles and says, "You think that's amazing! Wait until I manifest myself fully to you and share the secrets of the universe." We freeze in awe before such majesty and give thanks to the all-powerful One.

Acts 14:19–28
Psalm 145:10–11,12–13ab,21
John 14:27–31a

Wednesday

MAY 18

• ST. JOHN I, POPE AND MARTYR •

Anyone who does not remain in me
will be thrown out like a branch and wither;
people will gather them and throw them into a fire
and they will be burned.
—JOHN 15:6

A musician debuted a composition on today's Gospel
emphasizing the words about cutting off and throwing away.
It's much more comforting to focus on remaining in Christ, but
the songwriter accentuated being removed to invite listeners
to consider a more unsettling perspective on this passage.
When people listen during civil discourse to those whose
views aren't like theirs, they invite one another to consider
opposite points of view. One is not intrinsically better than
another. For some, punishment is an incentive to choose
rightly. Whatever leads to God is a move in the right direction.

Acts 15:1–6
Psalm 122:1–2,3–4ab,4cd–5
John 15:1–8

*And God, who knows the heart,
bore witness by granting them the Holy Spirit
just as he did us.*
—ACTS 15:8

One Christian denomination rejects drinking. Another insists that every issue must be spelled out in the Bible. Pope Francis caused shockwaves by saying, "Who am I to judge?" Meanwhile, God lavishly pours the Holy Spirit all around. The early church experienced conflicts over circumcision, strangled animals, and worship. Tempers flared. Yet they saw the Holy Spirit granted to communities in ways they never expected. Examining the fruits reveals the source. An example in our day is Christian rock music, often performed in megachurches where it draws huge crowds to hours of wildly exuberant prayer. God is praised, which indicates that the Spirit is at work. Audience members hold varying beliefs, but they unite to honor the Lord.

Acts 15:7–21
Psalm 96:1–2a,2b–3,10
John 15:9–11

[The letter said,] "We have with one accord decided to choose representatives."
—ACTS 15:25

Ever wonder what form of group discernment the leaders used to find unanimous agreement? Earlier in Acts they discussed and dissented. Therefore, it's unlikely they had a lightning bolt of insight. In the book *What's Your Decision? How to Make Choices with Confidence and Clarity*, the authors outline five pillars for sound decision making: discernment of spirits, a reflective (prayerful) mindset, the importance of emotional calm, getting help from others, and using the imagination to help consider the consequences of deciding one way or the other.

Acts 15:22–31
Psalm 57:8–9,10 and 12
John 15:12–17

Saturday
MAY 21

• ST. CHRISTOPHER MAGALLANES, PRIEST, AND COMPANIONS, MARTYRS •

Paul had [Timothy] circumcised,
for they all knew that [Timothy's] father was a Greek.
—ACTS 16:3B

It's uncommon in the Bible to identify a man by the women
in his life. Often the Bible skips even giving women's names
(Jairus's daughter, the widow of Nain, a hemorrhaging
woman, and Peter's mother-in-law). Timothy is known as
Eunice's son and Lois's grandson. Did they become Christians
before he did? Had Timothy's father banned circumcision for
his son while letting his Jewish wife raise Timothy in her
faith? In his biography of Paul, N.T. Wright suggests that
Timothy may have been circumcised so he could join Paul in
synagogues where Paul introduced Christ as Messiah the first
time. Imagine whether Timothy's mom or grandmother had
thought of this, how Timothy took the decision for
circumcision, or whether he thought of it himself.

Acts 16:1–10
Psalm 100:1b–2,3,5
John 15:18–21

*[Jesus said,] "If you loved me,
you would rejoice that I am going to the Father."*
—JOHN 14:28B

It's the Easter season, but we may not always feel joyful. It's a good time of year to cultivate joy by calling to memory or imagining things that bring pleasure, happiness, and spiritual joy. We can ask repeatedly for the grace of joy, especially when we feel down. What phrases bring happiness, pleasant memories, and holy enthusiasm? Here are a few suggestions: Heaven awaits! God is always loving! The sun is still shining. Gratitude lifts the spirits. God never lets us be tried beyond our strength. Consolations will return. Rejoice with singing! He's alive!

Acts 15:1–2,22–29
Psalm 67:2–3,5,6,8 (4)
Revelation 21:10–14,22–23
John 14:23–29

On the sabbath we went outside the city gate
along the river
where we thought there would be a place of prayer.
—ACTS 16:13B

Lydia speaks: In my travels, I've seen things few people see. Perhaps that's why women flock to me. It's not just my wealth or influence in Thyatira (formerly named Lydia by the way). I use my independent means for good and encouragement. My name means "kindred spirit." When Paul arrived at the river seeking a place of prayer, he found it in my heart. He didn't anticipate finding a physical place for prayer in my home! I prevailed; I just wouldn't take no for an answer, and Paul acquiesced. Eventually my house became the first place of prayer, the first church, in all of Europe. Yes, I'd say Paul found what he was looking for that day.

Acts 16:11–15
Psalm 149:1b–2,3–4,5–6a and 9b
John 15:26—16:4a

Tuesday

MAY 24

When I called, you answered me;
you built up strength within me.
—PSALM 138:3

When at the end of his rope again, all David could do was
pray, "Help!" It was enough. It's a remarkably effective prayer.
He admitted that he could not control everything. He saw
he was not in charge of his environment, family, workplace,
or church. What in this psalmist's admission most resonates
in this moment? God hopes that people surrender and admit
their need for a savior. God never fails. The psalmist is
strengthened for the next challenge, which sometimes comes
right on the heels of the last one. He knows—he
believes—that God will rescue him or give him graced
strength when he cries out for mercy.

Acts 16:22–34
Psalm 138:1–2ab,2cde–3,7c–8
John 16:5–11

Wednesday

MAY 25

[Jesus said,]
"I have much more to tell you, but you cannot
bear it now."
—JOHN 16:12

They say that God never gives you more than you can handle.
Two years ago today, George Floyd, a forty-six-year-old black
man, died in Minneapolis. Death defied the country's ability to
bear ugly sins made visible. Headlines highlighted a history of
racism denied and operating in secret. It felt like too much to
bear. And when protests morphed into riots, the United States
seemed at the breaking point. God is merciful even when sins
are egregious, but a message like that is difficult to hear during
strife. As Jesus approaches the cross again through broken
lives, he wants so much more for humanity than fear, anger,
and revenge.

Acts 17:15,22—18:1
Psalm 148:1–2,11–12,13,14
John 16:12–15

Thursday

MAY 26

• THE ASCENSION OF THE LORD •

"Why are you standing there looking at the sky?"
—ACTS 1:11A

The Feast of the Ascension is the perfect time to begin (if we haven't already) looking ahead and praying eagerly for the Holy Spirit to be poured afresh on our world. Pentecost is just a week from Sunday. We are full of anticipation during Advent, awaiting Christmas, and Lent is happily ended in Easter. How can we invoke and invite the feast of the great Advocate and Guide with as much enthusiasm? Better to look ahead than to continue looking up at an empty sky, wondering where Jesus is or has gone. Bringing the gaze back to eye level reveals that Jesus is still right here. Look in the face of someone who is poor. There is Jesus.

Acts 1:1–11
Psalm 47:2–3,6–7,8–9 (6)
Ephesians 1:17–23 or Hebrews 9:24–28; 10:19–23
Luke 24:46–53

Friday

MAY 27

• ST. AUGUSTINE OF CANTERBURY •

[Jesus said,] "Amen, amen, I say to you,
whatever you ask the Father in my name,
he will give you."
—JOHN 16:23

Ask. Keep asking. Don't stop asking. Don't give up. Ask in a different way. Ask in song, in penance, in fasting, and in tears. Ask in additional prayer time. Ask in silence. Ask by soliciting other voices to join you, especially those whose faith is even stronger than yours. Ask with hope of an answer that is for the greatest good. Ask from a stance of humility and submission to the will of the Most High. Ask from a body posture of pleading. Most important, ask in faith in the name of Jesus.

Acts 18:9–18
Psalm 47:2–3,4–5,6–7
John 16:20–23

All you peoples, clap your hands;
shout to God with cries of gladness.
—PSALM 47:2

What would it be like if people were to stand up and cheer at
Mass, right when the priest elevates the host, in adoration of
the great God Almighty? Crowds roar for a touchdown and
leap to their feet for an interception, so why not cry out in
jubilation to God in church? Can you just picture it? People
wearing JESUS TEAM gear, pulling out horns and jumping
up and down and hugging one another like it's a Super Bowl
win? The one, the only, Jesus Christ himself stands before us,
arms raised in celebration. The crowd goes wild. This is what
we've been hoping for. He's our reason for being. We are
seeing God incarnate, love in person. Doesn't that make you
want to cheer?

Acts 18:23–28
Psalm 47:2–3,8–9,10
John 16:23b–28

Sunday

MAY 29

• SEVENTH SUNDAY OF EASTER •

[Jesus said,] "Behold, I am coming soon."
—REVELATION 22:12

The Easter lilies are no longer blooming, and the alleluias
may have grown stale. The bright sunny days of spring's
consolations will soon slip into summer and vacations. The
words from Revelation hint that the Holy Spirit's big day is
coming up next week. This is no time to take a nap. Get
ready for wearing red and inviting a new Pentecost to take
hold. The Holy Spirit comes with power—overwhelmingly
merciful power. The Spirit brings awe and enthusiasm for
grace. And not only that. Jesus will return soon to take the
beloved to heaven. Are we ready?

Acts 7:55–60
Psalm 97:1–2, 6–7, 9
Revelation 22:12–14,16–17,20
John 17:20–26

[The believers answered,]
"We have never even heard that there is
a Holy Spirit."
—ACTS 19:2

Is it obvious from your life that the Holy Spirit exists? People see your behavior and make judgments about your beliefs and about what's important to you. If you invite the power of God's grace-giving Spirit into your daily life, the fruit will show in love, joy, peace, patience, kindness, goodness, self-control, gentleness, and faith. You don't receive the Holy Spirit in just a one-time shot at confirmation. People around you ought to see evidence of an ongoing injection of Spirit power. Is there something you can do today so people around you can't say they never even heard of God's dynamic Spirit?

Acts 19:1–8
Psalm 68:2–3ab,4–5acd,6–7ab
John 16:29–33

Tuesday

MAY 31

• THE VISITATION OF THE BLESSED VIRGIN MARY •

The King of Israel, the LORD, is in your midst;
you have no further misfortune to fear.
—ZEPHANIAH 3:15B

Now that's good, consoling news. How might we live aware
of that every waking moment? God sings joyfully over us. Of
course, the paradox of worldly troubles and sorrows causes
our enthusiasm to falter. But God's promises are unbreakable.
God is all powerful. A metaphor for God is *rock*. Think about
the solid, majestic granite monolith Half Dome, in Yosemite
National Park. Most hikers take twelve hours to scale it.
Compared to it, we're like fleas. So are the world's trials. We
cannot shake God's powerful devotion for us, even if we fly
as hard as we can against it. God prevails. Solid. Strong. Let's
sing for joy!

Zephaniah 3:14–18a or Romans 12:9–16
Isaiah 12:2–3,4bcd,5–6
Luke 1:39–56

As you sent me into the world,
so I sent them into the world.
—JOHN 17:18

Students graduating are sent into a new phase of their lives.
What kind of world will they enter? Just as in Jesus' day, the
world opposes much of what Christianity stands for because
society often values materialism to the point of idolatry,
personal comfort that dismisses others' needs, individualism
at the expense of community, and autonomy over the
common good. Movement into the world doesn't mean
becoming part of the dysfunction. What tools are needed to
stand up to values contrary to Christ? And what strengths?
Prayers for graduates might include intercessions that they
receive courage, patience, a willingness to be ridiculed for
choosing well, and a good sense of humor. Laughing at
adversity can assist in overcoming it. What else?

Acts 20:28–38
Psalm 68:29–30,33–35a,35bc–36ab
John 17:11b–19

Thursday

JUNE 2

• ST. MARCELLINUS AND ST. PETER, MARTYRS •

Father, they are your gift to me.
I wish that where I am they also may be with me.
—JOHN 17:24

Parents love giving presents to their children, and they especially love seeing their faces glow with joy and gratitude. Everywhere little Johnny goes, he wants that teddy bear right beside him. Try sending him to bed without it. You'll be searching all over the house to appease him. Jesus is not that kind of child, but he wants his people with him. You are a gift from God the Creator to his beloved Son. And Jesus wants to take you with him. It feels great to be so well loved.

Acts 22:30; 23:6–11
Psalm 16:1–2a and 5,7–8,9–10,11
John 17:20–26

Friday

JUNE 3

As far as the east is from the west,
so far has he put our transgressions from us.
—PSALM 103:12

How far *is* the east from the west? They never meet. Maybe
it's a metaphor for infinity. God sends our mistakes so far
away that we never need see them again. We're not meant to
return to or dredge them up again. When that happens, we
can suspect an enemy's hand in it; God isn't the one
reminding us of our sins. It could be our own inability to
forgive ourselves. If for some reason your past keeps nagging,
repeat a favorite hymn of praise to drive away that
temptation to dwell on past failings. Evil hates when we
praise God. Therefore, continue adoring God to make evil
desist. For now. Another tactic may surface. Stay awake.

Acts 25:13b–21
Psalm 103:1–2,11–12,19–20ab
John 21:15–19

Saturday

JUNE 4

The LORD is in his holy temple;
the LORD's throne is in heaven.
—PSALM 11:4

My rose bushes go crazy in May. I hate to throw out the
beautiful blooms when cut roses in the house droop. Using a
screen in the garage, I spread petals for drying. They will
look lovely later in bowls around the house. They make
scented token gifts when bagged. But my favorite use for
them mimics what will happen tomorrow in the Pantheon in
Rome on Pentecost. Rose petals dropped through the oculus
flutter down on the people like tongues of fire. I throw rose
petals, as if I'm a flower girl at a wedding, only I toss them in
the air and watch them flutter down on friends and family.
How might you tangibly celebrate the Holy Spirit whom
God lavishes upon us?

Acts 28:16–20,30–31
Psalm 11:4,5 and 7
John 21:20–25

Sunday

JUNE 5

• PENTECOST SUNDAY •

*Yet we hear them speaking in our own tongues
of the mighty acts of God.*
—ACTS 2:11B

The Spirit is not given to be hoarded. Imagine that you, in this moment, are suddenly infused with the kind of powerful Spirit that emboldened the people in that upper room on Pentecost. What might you post on social media, text, or email? Who would you call, and what would you say? As the second reading says, you have no more reasons to fear, no matter what suffering or ridicule lie ahead. Today isn't just about birthday cake and celebrating the past.

There's a new birthday of the church whenever the Spirit chooses. Be bold. Share that cake outside your normal circle. Dare to let the Holy Spirit set you on fire.

VIGIL:
Genesis 11:1–9 or Exodus 19:3–8a,16–20b
or Ezekiel 37:1–4 or Joel 3:1–5
Psalm 104:1–2,24,35,27–28,29,30
Romans 8:22–27
John 7:37–39

DAY:
Acts 2:1–11
Psalm 104:1,24,29–30,31,34
1 Corinthians 12:3b–7,12–13 or Romans
8:8–17
John 20:19–23 or 14:15–16,23b–26

Monday

JUNE 6

• THE BLESSED VIRGIN MARY, MOTHER OF THE CHURCH •

All these devoted themselves with one accord to prayer, together with some women, and Mary the mother of Jesus, and his brothers.
—ACTS 1:14

Spontaneous prayer seems to come naturally to some. Others need practice to cultivate the skill of being a good conversationalist with God. Mary could teach what she knew about prayer; she was keenly attuned to God through her relationship with her son and his father. She already knew what it was like to be overcome by God's Spirit because she experienced it at the Annunciation. Mary was a powerful force in the days leading up to and including the descent of the Holy Spirit, who had already showered her with the graces needed to parent Jesus. It's easier to learn prayer from an expert and to be committed when you have the support of others. Mary's experiences made her a great teacher and midwife for the birth of the early church.

Genesis 3:9–15, 20 or Acts 1:12–14
Psalm 87:1–2, 3 and 5, 6–7
John 19:25–34

JUNE 7

*[Jesus said,] "You are the light of the world.
A city set on a mountain cannot be hidden."*
—MATTHEW 5:14

Fumbling in the dark under the desk, I couldn't plug in the cable. I gave up trying without a flashlight. I opened the powerful beam on my phone to light the spot bright as day. An impossible task was quickly complete. I also discovered some paper clips, dust balls, and dead bugs I wish I hadn't seen. Bright light reveals more than I expect. The same is true in my spiritual life. Jesus said, "I am the light," and he wants me to be that, too. In God's brilliant light I discover things I neglected and need to clean up. And the light is *love*. Maybe I notice someone struggling in desolation. God calls me to use Christ's powerful love-light to illuminate the way.

1 Kings 17:7–16
Psalm 4:2–3,4–5,7b–8
Matthew 5:13–16

Wednesday

JUNE 8

*Seeing this, all the people fell prostrate and said,
"The LORD is God! The LORD is God!"*
—1 KINGS 18:39

What would it take in this day and age to cause us to fall on
the ground and praise God effusively? Technology serves up
so many wonders that little impresses us anymore. Today's
first reading is quite dramatic. We can imagine the scene: fire
from heaven incinerates everything, even the stones. What
would a theophany look like in our day? Perhaps God is
dramatically revealed and we are too busy to notice, or we
explain it away scientifically, or we invent some plausible
explanation. Faith like Elijah's is a magnet. Is there someone
close to God who can point to the Most High's actions today
in ways that cause us to tremble in awe?

1 Kings 18:20–39
Psalm 16:1b–2ab,4,5ab and 8,11
Matthew 5:17–19

Thursday

JUNE 9

• ST. EPHREM OF SYRIA, DEACON AND DOCTOR OF THE CHURCH •

You have crowned the year with your bounty,
and your paths overflow with a rich harvest;
The untilled meadows overflow with it.
and rejoicing clothes the hills.
—PSALM 65:12–13

People who undertake the *Spiritual Exercises* in everyday life, also known as the *Nineteenth Annotation*, often wrap up their year-long adventure around now. For eight or nine months they have contemplated love and marveled at the truth that all good things descend from above. As the psalm says, rejoicing covers the hills completely. An abundant harvest results from a year-long commitment to structured time with the Lord. If you've never tried the Exercises you might wish to look into it. You may find the next liturgical year royally crowned with God's bounteous love and graces.

1 Kings 18:41–46
Psalm 65:10,11,12–13
Matthew 5:20–26

Friday

JUNE 10

Jesus said to his disciples,
"You have heard that it was said,
You shall not commit adultery.
But I say to you,
everyone who looks at a woman with lust
has already committed adultery with her
in his heart."
—MATTHEW 5:27–28

Some days I feel like smacking my husband over some aggravation. I'd never do it! In those moments I take for granted the blessings of marriage. In truth, I dread the thought of being called to widowhood. I know no one who wants this vocation, which is thrust upon people. Sins of disrespect for my husband do neither of us any good. Matrimony is a sacrament that offers special graces, and I need to remember to request them from our generous God, who wants to use us as a sign of love in our hurting world.

1 Kings 19:9a,11–16
Psalm 27:7–8a,8b–9abc,13–14
Matthew 5:27–32

Saturday

JUNE 11

• ST. BARNABAS, APOSTLE •

*Then [Barnabas] went to Tarsus to look for Saul, and when he had
found him he brought him to Antioch. For a whole year they met with
the church and taught a large number of people, and it was in Antioch
that the disciples were first called Christians.*

—ACTS 11:25-26

Paul escaped Jews conspiring to kill him in Damascus only to
find on arrival in Jerusalem that everyone was afraid of him.
Barnabas stepped up and vouched for Paul. Some believe
they were friends previously from studying Judaic law.
Whatever their relationship, the two traveled and worked
extensively together and relied on each other. They didn't
always agree, but their missionary work was powerful. The
results were a strong community at Antioch. What friends
encourage me to pursue Christ's mandate to bring about the
reign of God?

Acts 11:21b–26; 13:1–3
Psalm 98:1,2–3ab,3cd–4,5–6
Matthew 5:33–37

JUNE 12

• THE MOST HOLY TRINITY •

I was his delight day by day,
playing before him all the while.
—PROVERBS 8:30

God holds the universe in balance. God is also Abba,
willingly spending time with and enjoying people's company.
God's Spirit of Wisdom celebrated creation while it was
being formed. God had and still has fun with it. Look how
good and lovable everything is, the Almighty says to God's
self, even now. A small child at play laughs and takes her
time with a mud pie or chalk drawing. She willingly sees
good all around her. God's Trinitarian presence is
unfathomable but also delightful. The triune One plays on
the earth and is entertained by its mountains, oceans, and
core, as well as the myriad creatures that populate it. "Will
you come out and play?" says the Creator/Brother/
Wisdom/Friend.

Proverbs 8:22–31
Psalm 8:4–5,6–7,8–9 (2a)
Romans 5:1–5
John 16:12–15

Monday

JUNE 13

He has sent me to bring glad tidings to the lowly,
to heal the brokenhearted.
—ISAIAH 61:1

St. Anthony is known to come through when people lose things. But he isn't a doctor of the church for his detective abilities. Nor is being a contemporary of St. Francis of Assisi the reason he's remembered. His eloquent preaching, drawing huge crowds, revealed a grasp of Christ's message applied to everyday life. He is credited with saying that charity is the soul of faith and makes it alive; without love, faith dies. And that the devil is afraid of us when we pray and make sacrifices. He lived in imitation of Christ, bringing joyful tidings to the lowly. All followers of Christ are called today to boldly, joyfully, share the Good News as he did. Loving words console hurting hearts.

MEMORIAL
Isaiah 61:1-3d
Psalm 89:2-3,4-5,21-22, 25 and 27
Luke 10:1-9

Thoroughly wash me from my guilt
and of my sin cleanse me.
—PSALM 51:4

God doesn't always answer my prayers. Why? What is God seeing that I'm not? An image of a muddy child running to her mother for a hug pops into mind. Seeing the mess, Mother laughs, holds the child at arm's length, lifts her up, and plunks her into a bathtub. The child protests at first, kicking and screaming. Soon the water is welcome; the child relaxes into the cleansing bath. Mother knew just what was needed. First the mud had to be washed away before it was time to approach another person for a hug. Sometimes I go to God in prayer and the answer is, "Not just yet, dear. There's something we need to do first."

1 Kings 21:17–29
Psalm 51:3–4,5–6ab,11 and 16
Matthew 5:43–48

*[Jesus said,] "When you pray, go to your inner room,
close the door, and pray to your Father in secret."*
—MATTHEW 6:6

Where is the inner room in your life? It might be your car on
autopilot heading to work, where you listen to prayerful
music. Maybe it's a favorite chair at home where you sit
undisturbed, gazing out a window at natural beauty. The
meeting place with God might be a chapel during a quick
stop before the Blessed Sacrament. It could be all of these,
plus a secret hideout that only you and your best friend Jesus
know about. Your room really is within. You can go there at
any time and wait, knowing that God will eventually arrive.
It's your special place, where you are free to cry, coax, or
commiserate. It's a safe and private space in which you can be
fully heard and loved.

2 Kings 2:1,6–14
Psalm 31:20,21,24
Matthew 6:1–6,16–18

Thursday

JUNE 16

[Jesus said,] "Your Father knows what you need before you ask him."
—MATTHEW 6:8

In a convent somewhere, a cloistered nun reviews news headlines and prays for you, though she doesn't know it's you who needs her prayers today. But you're affected by world events, and her prayers therefore include you. Countless intercessions have lifted you when you didn't know it: teachers, elderly relatives now dead, and casual observers who watched you wiggle during church when you were small. A stranger who saw you drive erratically prayed for your safety. A passerby prayed for you as you stood downcast at a signal. No prayer is ever wasted. You will never know this side of heaven who has prayed for you. But you can take a moment right now to pray for those who have prayed for you during your lifetime.

Sirach 48:1–14
Psalm 97:1–2,3–4,5–6,7
Matthew 6:7–15

Friday
JUNE 17

[Jesus said,] "For where your treasure is, there also will your heart be."
—MATTHEW 6:21

At the Tower of London, a conveyor belt moves visitors past walls painted black, which focus attention on ancient coronets and scepters that dazzle brightly in the targeted overhead lighting. Before long, the visitor is outside again. The tour doesn't last, nor did the earthly lives of the royalty who once wore these jewels, which belong to someone else now. True wealth is knowing God and serving wherever God leads, which is discernable through an attitude detached from wealth, success, or even long life. Spiritual freedom allows the voice of inspiration to be heard. God made humans to love and praise the one almighty Creator. Everything on earth is here to help people reach this purpose: to find true fortune in Christ and the gospel of love.

2 Kings 11:1–4,9–18,20
Psalm 132:11,12,13–14,17–18
Matthew 6:19–23

[Jesus asked,] "Can any of you by worrying add a single moment to your life-span?"
—MATTHEW 6:27

Jesus' words are consoling but quickly forgotten when the dog goes missing because somebody left the back door open. With a teen in tears on the phone, a mother makes a U-turn and rushes home, more concerned for the teen than the dog who will soon find his way back. "Worrying is paying a debt you don't owe," Mark Twain said. But it's still so easy to do! Today's passage goes on for ten verses, trying to help us stop habits of worry. Life is more than good health, wealth, honors, a long life, and so on. It's normal to be attached to a beloved pet, and mothers will stress about teens, but Jesus commands us to quit worrying. Whatever we face, God is there, loving.

2 Chronicles 24:17–25
Psalm 89:4–5,29–30,31–32,33–34
Matthew 6:24–34

Sunday

JUNE 19

• THE MOST HOLY BODY AND BLOOD OF CHRIST (CORPUS CHRISTI) •

[The Lord said,] "You are a priest forever, according to the order
of Melchizedek."
—PSALM 110:4

In the baptismal liturgy, we are anointed to be priests,
prophets, and kings. The oil marks us indelibly, just as it does
a favorite shirt. That oil cannot be removed, making us
clearly identifiable when we reach heaven's door. What
qualities make us priests today, as well as forever? An
ordained priest makes Christ truly present on the altar and
distributes Christ to others. When we love through our
actions, Christ is truly present, and we distribute the reality
of our Savior to others. Priesthood isn't about power, control,
or hierarchy. Priesthood is defined by humble service to the
people God loves. Our common priesthood mediates
between God and others through teaching, worship, and
everyday leadership (*Catechism of the Catholic Church*, #1592).

Genesis 14:18–20
Psalm 110:1,2,3,4 (4b)
1 Corinthians 11:23–26
Luke 9:11b–17

Monday

JUNE 20

They did not listen, but were as stiff-necked
as their fathers,
who had not believed in the LORD, their God.
—2 KINGS 17:14

I woke with a neck so tight I could barely turn my head. A
heating pad helped, but my rigid muscles resisted. I could see
only straight ahead unless I moved my whole body. It took
time and slow, cautious movements for the muscles to give
way. Being stiff-necked was uncomfortable. I looked pitiful. A
spiritual rigidity sets in when I refuse to be open to God's
love. If only I would plug into the power of God and let the
fiery flames of the Holy Spirit warm my soul. I want to
unlearn the paralyzing assumptions that freeze my
movements so that I can serve those in need with compassion
and without judgment.

2 Kings 17:5–8,13–15a,18
Psalm 60:3,4–5,12–13
Matthew 7:1–5

Great is the LORD and wholly to be praised.
—PSALM 48:2

Praising and appreciating God lead to a happy heart. A woman of ninety-plus years who was confined to assisted living said, "I'm making miracles every day." How could a frail, wheelchair-bound old woman be a miracle worker? "Every day I see miracles, just looking out the window," she explained. A leaf blowing, a worker passing, and a car speeding by were all miracles to her and reasons to praise God. She prayed constantly, and she felt privileged to have problems sleeping. For her, it was an invitation to pray. "Hooray! I'm awake!" she would say to herself. She loved every bit of her life, limited though it was in a million ways. To her, every circumstance was a reason to praise God.

2 Kings 19:9b–11,14–21,31–35a,36
Psalm 48:2–3ab,3cd–4,10–11
Matthew 7:6,12–14

$\mathcal{W}ednesday$

JUNE 22

• ST. PAULINUS OF NOLA, BISHOP • ST. JOHN FISHER, BISHOP, AND ST.
THOMAS MORE, MARTYRS •

And all the people stood as participants in the covenant.
—2 KINGS 23:3B

The scene is graphic. Imagine you're the king, completely
unaware of the book the priest found. Reading it, you realize
that your subjects have committed heinous crimes. In grief
you rip your clothes to shreds. You expect God's blazing
anger and beg the priest to pray. Despite feeling terrible, you
go to the temple and listen as the entire contents of the lost
book are read aloud. The entire book! The people stand rapt
as they listen. Representing them, you recommit to God's
unbreakable covenant. "People!" you cry out. "It's a new day.
From now on, we *will* follow the Lord, with our whole hearts
and souls! No exceptions." What would you do next if you
were king? What will you do today?

2 Kings 22:8–13; 23:1–3
Psalm 119:33,34,35,36,37,40
Matthew 7:15–20

Thursday

JUNE 23

• THE NATIVITY OF ST. JOHN THE BAPTIST •

*[Y]ou will have joy and gladness, and many will rejoice at his birth, for
he will be great in the sight of the Lord.*
—LUKE 1:14–15

Birthdays cause great celebrations, and gratitude is especially
deep for parents who've struggled to conceive. Today is a
great opportunity to pray for couples who have endured
miscarriages. The death of any child creates a deep sadness,
but when it occurs before birth, it is an especially painful and
often hidden grief. The percentage of pregnancies ending in
miscarriages is higher than most people realize because so
many suffer in silence. Many women feel movement in the
womb, as Elizabeth did with John, only to lose the child
before birth. Longing for life is a powerful yearning. May
those of us already alive pray to be joyful every time we have
the privilege of a birthday.

VIGIL:	DAY:
Jeremiah 4:1–10	Isaiah 49:1–6
Psalm 71:1–2,3–4a,5–6ab,15ab and 17	Psalm 139:1b–3,13–14ab,14c–15
1 Peter 1:8–12	Acts 13:22–26
Luke 1:5–17	Luke 1:57–66,80

Friday

JUNE 24

• THE MOST SACRED HEART OF JESUS •

God proves his love for us in that while we were still sinners Christ died for us.
—ROMANS 5:8

In 1672, St. Margaret Mary Alacoque began having visions of Jesus, whose desire to establish peace in our homes, to comfort us in afflictions, and to be our secure refuge in life and at the hour of death, was so strong she could see his heart bursting from his chest. Jesus made it clear that he wanted to bestow abundant blessing on us and all we endeavor to do. Faced with God's offer of infinite mercy, how can we stay lukewarm? We are rescued from cloudy and dark places by overwhelming love and concern. Today's readings with images of sheep focus not on our worthiness but on rescue. While we are lost, undeserving, and still sinners, God loves us.

Ezekiel 34:11–16
Psalm 23:1–3a,3b–4,5,6 (1)
Romans 5:5b–11
Luke 15:3–7

JUNE  25

• THE IMMACULATE HEART OF THE BLESSED VIRGIN MARY •

His mother said to him, "Son, why have you done this to us? Your father and I have been looking for you with great anxiety."
—LUKE 2:48

Anxiety afflicts the best of us, even the model disciple Mary. Chances are that Jesus' parents endured many worrisome moments as their son grew and learned. Kids don't come with instruction manuals. Imagine the fear of having lost the Son of God. What inner dialogue might Mary or Joseph have had with God? These questions might help: "What do you expect from me? Why give me such a terrible responsibility? Have I gotten in your plan's way?" How might God reassure them? Doubts must have arisen as they searched for days. You may have doubts about your role in God's plan. Have you felt overwhelmed by responsibility or thwarted in what you thought God wanted for you? Talk to Jesus about that now.

Lamentations 2:2, 10–14, 18–19
Psalm 74: 1b–2, 3–5, 6–7, 20–21
Luke 2:41–51

For you were called for freedom, brothers and sisters.
—GALATIANS 5:13

The Principle and Foundation offered by St. Ignatius in the
Spiritual Exercises invites retreatants to be free from anything
that pulls them away from God. Occasionally it's good for
retreatants to devote an *examen* (a prayerful review of the day
from God's point of view) to assessing where they have
behaved with genuine freedom during the past week, and
when the yoke of slavery reappeared, to use Paul's metaphor.
Desires for riches, success, and accolades can sneak up over
time and steal peace. God invites disciples to be attached only
to the Trinity, who always loves. Freedom from worldly
attachments feels liberating. So does expressing gratitude.

1 Kings 19:16b,19–21
Psalm 16:1–2,5,7–8,9–10,11
Galatians 5:1,13–18
Luke 9:51–62

"When you do these things, shall I be deaf to it?
Or do you think that I am like yourself?"
—PSALM 50:21

Any image of God will fall short of who God really is. Today's readings call into question old notions, such as a hands-off Creator. Is the Almighty a demanding father with exceedingly high standards for human behavior? A judgmental scorekeeper pulling strings from on high? Is God a *He*? Must humanity be wary because God can crush it with a glance? Is God made in the image and likeness of humanity, instead of the other way around? While the Hebrew Scriptures offer some disturbing images, the truth of God is manifest in Jesus. Yet Jesus speaks cryptically at times. Let's pray for the grace today not to be deaf to the call of our Abba God.

Amos 2:6–10,13–16
Psalm 50:16bc–17,18–19,20–21,22–23
Matthew 8:18–22

"What sort of man is this,
whom even the winds and the sea obey?"
—MATTHEW 8:27

Mark's account says that other boats were with Jesus' boat.
What might it be like to contemplate being in one of those
other boats? You don't see Jesus in your stern, but you sure
see the storm. No wonder you feel afraid and doubt that you
really witnessed miraculous cures just a few hours ago.
Maybe there are natural explanations for those. Maybe you
fall on your knees in this boat, begging for help because
you're dying out here. You've been through storms, but none
like this. What kind of leader points people directly into a
storm and then seems absent? It's more than you can bear.
How can you trust when things look dire? "Patience," God
whispers into your soul. Suddenly, you see Jesus stand up in
the other boat. He raises his arms.

Amos 3:1–8; 4:11–12
Psalm 5:4b–6a,6b–7,8
Matthew 8:23–27

J U N E · 2 9

• ST. PETER AND ST. PAUL, APOSTLES •

[Peter said,] "Now I know for certain
that the Lord sent his angel
and rescued me."
—ACTS 12:11

Faith demands belief in the implausible. Here's a
"CliffsNotes" version of this story: Suddenly a spirit was
there, tapping Peter. "Get up quickly." Chains fell. The angel
said, "Follow me." Peter assumed he was dreaming. They
headed down an alley. The angel left; Peter recovered his
senses. Rhoda forgot to open the gate when Peter arrived
because she was so incredulous. She ran to tell the others.
"You're out of your mind," they told her. Peter kept knocking.
Amazing! Wouldn't you like to participate in a community
where miracles like these happen! Perhaps you do.

VIGIL:
Acts 3:1–10
Psalm 19:2–3,4–5
Galatians 1:11–20
John 21:15–19

DAY:
Acts 12:1–11
Psalm 34:2–3,4–5,6–7,8–9
2 Timothy 4:6–8,17–18
Matthew 16:13–19

Thursday

JUNE 30

When the crowds saw this they were struck with awe
and glorified God who had given
such authority.
—MATTHEW 9:8

What's more awe-inspiring in my life: sins forgiven or a
miraculous cure? A recent experience of the sacrament of
reconciliation was so powerful for me that I glorified God for
the freedom from shackles on my soul. Outwardly, nothing
looked different, and there was no mat to pick up. Still the
consolations I felt were compelling. Through a priest's gentle
voice, a divine invitation sent me forth to sin no more. I
accepted a comforting fresh start. I left past mistakes behind.
Jesus, thank you for giving me courage and using endearing
names for me, like "my child." When was the last time you
enjoyed the graces of this sacrament? Schedule with a wise
and trustworthy confessor today.

Amos 7:10–17
Psalm 19:8,9,10,11
Matthew 9:1–8

[Jesus said,] "Go and learn the meaning of the words,
I desire mercy, not sacrifice.
I did not come to call the righteous but sinners."
—MATTHEW 9:13

It's tempting to point a finger, like a Pharisee, at people whose religious, political, or other stance is opposed to ours. Jesus addressed Pharisees when telling the prodigal son parable. The older brother wants to see sinners punished, not given mercy. Mercy is a complex virtue and grace. Perhaps the Pharisees in the audience saw themselves in that older brother. Were they moved to question their way of being? Are we? Mercy includes compassion, forgiveness, and an assumption that it's in another's power to grant it. Mercy is godlike. Several popular litanies use the response, "Have mercy on us." Perhaps a better antiphon is *thank you, God, for having mercy on us.*

Amos 8:4–6,9–12
Psalm 119:2,10,20,30,40,131
Matthew 9:9–13

Kindness and truth shall meet;
justice and peace shall kiss.
—PSALM 85:11

Psalm 85 begins with begging for divine favor. Is God going to stay mad for generations? asks the psalmist. "I will listen for what God, the LORD, has to say" (Psalm 85:9). The writer immediately moves to God's response, and as a result, hope intervenes. It's the same hope we'll hear again when this psalm appears during Advent's second week. Peace kissing justice is a hopeful promise amid adversity. Think of an example in your life where opposites existed side by side. Peace and justice don't always occur together. Nor do truth and kindness always meet among people, but they meet in Jesus. Now there's a strong reason for looking to the future with joy. Heaven is ours. Evil doesn't win.

Amos 9:11–15
Psalm 85:9ab and 10,11–12,13–14
Matthew 9:14–17

As a mother comforts her child,
so will I comfort you.
—ISAIAH 66:13

Watching the skin-to-skin contact between my daughter and her two-week-old daughter as she breastfed, I almost felt like an intruder witnessing a very intimate, unique, and profound experience. Love and connection were tangible. It reminded me of a time when my mother was hospitalized; I was in about the sixth grade, and I felt very afraid. Mom invited me to sit on the side of her bed, and she pulled my head to her ample breast. I will never forget her softness and how comforted I felt in that trying time. God is like a mother carrying me in her arms, caressing me on her lap, where I am comforted in a personal and private space. May we suck fully of the milk of God, who nourishes us with Christ's own body and blood.

Isaiah 66:10–14c
Psalm 66:1–3,4–5,6–7,16,20 (1)
Galatians 6:14–18
Luke 10:1–12,17–20 or 10:1–9

Thus says the LORD:
I will allure her;
I will lead her into the desert
and speak to her heart.
—HOSEA 2:16

Do you feel this way in your relationship with God? On the heels of yesterday, the church offers another surprisingly intimate metaphor for how God feels about you. Think about a time when you felt pulled toward God. Consider where, when, and how this occurred. If you can't pinpoint a specific instance when you felt drawn into a deserted place where God spoke to your heart, ask for this blessing right now. Give yourself the gift of ten minutes alone. Perhaps go into a closet and shut the door so that all outer stimuli are removed. Be present in the dark desert of time. Ask God for the grace of a personal encounter with the person of Jesus.

Hosea 2:16,17c–18,21–22
Psalm 145:2–3,4–5,6–7,8–9
Matthew 9:18–26

Tuesday

JULY 5

Jesus went around . . .
curing every disease and illness. At the sight of the crowds, his heart was
moved with pity for them because they were troubled and abandoned, like
sheep without a shepherd.
—MATTHEW 9:35–36

Listen to the mute man talking a mile a minute as he tells
you, a friend in his town, about the healing: "Praise to God,
who sent the Messiah! You should've heard the gasp from the
crowd. The first words out of my mouth were praises, and I
just can't stop them. I literally jumped for joy. People stared.
My sister, who's the one who brought me to Jesus, hugged
me so hard I couldn't breathe. Oh! I'd been chained so long
that my tongue hurt. I want to tell everyone about Jesus! And
guess what, Jesus didn't heal just some. He heals everyone."

Hosea 8:4–7,11–13
Psalm 115:3–4,5–6,7ab–8,9–10
Matthew 9:32–38

Sing to [God], sing his praise,
proclaim all his wondrous deeds.
—PSALM 105:2

Return to the Gospel meditation scene from yesterday, where
you were a villager in conversation with the man Jesus
healed. Today the man is teaching you praises that you've
never memorized before. He sets them to music to help you
remember. You gape and give glory without embarrassment
as you let yourself go in praise of God. Thanks to the
instruction from this man, you decide on your next, perhaps
radical, step in following Jesus. What will it be? How will
you look to the Lord who is stronger than anything, and how
will you serve Jesus constantly?

Hosea 10:1–3,7–8,12
Psalm 105:2–3,4–5,6–7
Matthew 10:1–7

[Jesus said,] "*Cure the sick, raise the dead,
cleanse the lepers, drive out demons.
Without cost you have received; without cost
you are to give.*"
—MATTHEW 10:8

How do we fulfill this mandate from Jesus in 2022? Every Christian, at one time or another, has participated in miracles, but perhaps not as often as we should. And we probably underestimate the wonders we perform. We take people to doctor appointments, fill prescriptions, make tea and healthy meals, and cure the sick as a result. We sit with someone grieving, helping them raise up from debilitating sorrow. Through a kind word we cleanse a person who is treated like a leper in society. Insidious evil sneaks into our television programming, so we turn it off. We contentedly serve and volunteer, expecting no paycheck. These, too, are miracles. We pay our blessings forward.

Hosea 11:1–4,8e–9
Psalm 80:2ac and 3b,15–16
Matthew 10:7–15

I will heal their defection, says the LORD,
I will love them freely.
—HOSEA 14:5

The prophet compares you to a plant that will flower like lilies. If you ever get stuck thinking that God in the Hebrew Scriptures is a meanie or a punisher, then try verses of consolation like these. God wants so much good for you, such that you become like a mighty tree with deep, strong roots. God is like dew, covering everything with life-giving water. Positive metaphors for God fill Scripture, like healing balm on an open sore. God wants you to be so fruitful that others will find shelter under your branches, and who knows, even make apple pies out of your abundant harvest. God has high hopes. What do you think is God's dream for you? God cares about your opinion and wants to work *with* you, through your deepest desires.

Hosea 14:2–10
Psalm 51:3–4,8–9,12–13,14 and 17
Matthew 10:16–23

Saturday

JULY 9

• ST. AUGUSTINE ZHAO RONG, PRIEST, AND COMPANIONS, MARTYRS •

Even all the hairs of your head are counted.
So do not be afraid; you are worth more
than many sparrows.
—MATTHEW 10:30–31

Tom is mostly bald, or as he says, "follically" challenged, and he has a series of jokes to show how comfortable he is with his lot. "God made a few perfect heads," he says, "and the rest he covered with hair." I think he makes it easy on God because my brother has fewer hairs for God to number. Tom also says that grass doesn't grow on a busy street. Seriously, though, God knows all and overlooks nothing, not even the smallest bacteria. So why do I worry? Because I forgot a very basic truth: God has everything under control and loves all of creation, whether it has 100,000 hairs or none.

Isaiah 6:1–8
Psalm 93:1ab,1cd–2,5
Matthew 10:24–33

JULY 10

• FIFTEENTH SUNDAY IN ORDINARY TIME •

Jesus said to him, "Go and do likewise."
—LUKE 10:37

Here's a man who could quote the rules and never would
want to violate a commandment. His follow-up question to
Jesus may have indicated a desire for something more.
Perhaps the scholar was debating someone and wanted
justification for his argument. His request for clarification
could be an opening to deeper humility, and a more generous
way of loving. Jesus turns a request for a definition into an
invitation to wade a little deeper into what God wants.
Spend a few moments considering how the scholar may have
acted after this.

Deuteronomy 30:10–14
Psalm 69:14,17,30–31,33–34,36,37 or Ps 19: 8, 9, 10, 11
Colossians 1:15–20
Luke 10:25–37

Wash yourselves clean!
Put away your misdeeds from before my eyes;
cease doing evil; learn to do good.
—ISAIAH 1:16–17

Isaiah hears God plead for proactivity. It's not enough for Israel to wring its hands and offer empty pleas. It's time for action—to begin with, turning from wrongdoing, even on a small scale. Bad behaviors need to give way to caring acts of service toward those most in need. For a person going from one sin to the next, the good Spirit stings consciences with remorse. Isaiah advises his listeners to use their remorse as an impetus to do good rather than merely rant about what's wrong with the world.

Isaiah 1:10–17
Psalm 50:8–9,16bc–17,21 and 23
Matthew 10:34—11:1

Take care you remain tranquil and do not fear;
let not your courage fail.
—ISAIAH 7:4

When Isaiah told Ahaz this message from God, unfortunately the king didn't listen. He relied on his preconceived opinions and plans. Big mistake. He ended up a vassal to a foreign leader. How many times does God have to tell people to stay steady, be at peace, and not let overwhelming odds against them cause them to falter! A million, maybe, because the same must be said again today. God allows people to make free (and dumb) choices, but God also can work with the results and bring about good every time (although in some cases it seems to take a really long time).

Isaiah 7:1–9
Psalm 48:2–3a,3b–4,5–6,7–8
Matthew 11:20–24

JULY 13

For the LORD will not cast off his people,
nor abandon his inheritance;
But judgment shall again be with justice,
and all the upright of heart shall follow it.
—PSALM 94:14–15

My parents could stop us kids in our tracks with a glance. We called it the "death look." They didn't need to say anything. We knew what we'd done. And we stopped doing it, as if we were playing freeze tag. That's the game where if "it" tags you, you freeze in place until someone not yet frozen touches you. We knew the household rules, and we knew how to follow them. We also knew how to judge ourselves justly when caught by that look. We were never cast off. In fact, sometimes the death look suddenly switched into uncontrollable laughter. We were so loved.

Isaiah 10:5–7,13b–16
Psalm 94:5–6,7–8,9–10,14–15
Matthew 11:25–27

Thursday

JULY 14

• ST. KATERI TEKAKWITHA, VIRGIN •

*[Jesus said to the crowds:] "Come to me, all you who labor and
are burdened,
and I will give you rest."*
—MATTHEW 11:28

Imagine all your worries loaded into a wagon. How big does
the wagon need to be? Is it a Red Flyer or farm-sized? The
wagon is pulled by chains, and you're dragging it. You are at
the foot of a hill, and at the top of it Jesus sits on a large
rock, looking to the horizon ahead. As you pull the wagon
up to Jesus, he turns and smiles. He invites you to drop the
chains at his feet. Perhaps you will need Jesus to help you
remove the chains. Jesus slides over so you can sit down next
to him and look ahead at the horizon together. What do you
see and hear as you rest with Jesus there?

Isaiah 26:7–9,12,16–19
Psalm 102:13–14ab and 15,16–18,19–21
Matthew 11:28–30

[Hezekiah prayed,] "O LORD, remember how faithfully
and wholeheartedly
I conducted myself in your presence,
doing what was pleasing to you!"
—ISAIAH 38:3

Hezekiah takes stock of his behavior and pleads for mercy, which God grants. Was it necessary for Judah's king to examine his life before God would show mercy? As sometimes happens, God allows a soul to struggle so that the person can get a better sense of their worth or strength, or lack thereof. "If you do not know your own dignity and condition, you cannot value anything at its proper worth," St. Bonaventure wrote in *Holiness of Life*.

Isaiah 38:1–6,21–22,7–8
Isaiah 38:10,11,12abcd,16
Matthew 12:1–8

Saturday

JULY 16

• OUR LADY OF MOUNT CARMEL •

*[Mary said,] "My soul proclaims the greatness of the Lord,
my spirit rejoices in God my savior."*
—LUKE 1:46

What would it take to live a grace-filled day today? Is there a
specific grace you wish you had? Did you ask for it? God is
listening. The first grace needed for a grace-filled day is
gratitude. It's foundational! If you feel grateful, that itself is
God's gift. Mary's words pour forth praise; they are a form of
gratitude, too. And the opposite of gratitude just might be
complaining. "God, give more, or different, or better."
Cultivate an attitude that gives thanks for the surprising
blessings that come disguised as problems. Like Mary, look
on the bright side. She could have felt woe at being poor,
pregnant, and unwed. Instead, she focused on gratitude that
the Messiah was on the way.

MEMORIAL
Zechariah 2:14–17
Luke 1:46–47, 48–49, 50–51, 52–53, 54–55
Matthew 12:46–50

*Jesus entered a village
where a woman whose name was Martha
welcomed him.*
—LUKE 10:38

Luke focuses on Martha's welcome, not on her brother Lazarus's. That's unusual for first-century accounts, which focus on the man of a house. Mary is mentioned in relationship to Martha, who is the star of this reading. Imagine what might have happened next. When Jesus told Martha that Mary chose better by listening to him instead of worrying, did Martha say, "Okay! I will choose the better part too"? Did she flop down with Mary at the feet of Christ, let go of worry, and wait until Jesus led the way into the kitchen and they all cooked together? If you put yourself into this scene, what do you see and hear? What would Christ say to you? Would his tone be reprimanding or endearing?

Genesis 18:1–10a
Psalm 15:2–3,3–4,5 (1a)
Colossians 1:24–28
Luke 10:38–42

O my people, what have I done to you,
or how have I wearied you? Answer me!
—MICAH 6:3

Some of the readings this week leave me feeling like I'm in Lent, not Ordinary Time. I hear the words of a Good Friday hymn in Micah, and Jesus needs to chastise his beloved Jewish leaders in the Gospel. God laments again. With all the disobedience, disbelief, and contrariness among the people of Israel, God has every right to smite them, generation after generation. Evil and unfaithful generations seek proof. Strangely, this gives me hope. I look around my world and see injustice endemic to society. We are steeped in a depraved era, and yet God stands close by. God never fails to love. God never wearies of forgiving.

Micah 6:1–4,6–8
Psalm 50:5–6,8–9,16bc–17,21 and 23
Matthew 12:38–42

Tuesday

JULY 19

Someone told [Jesus], "Your mother and your brothers
are standing outside."
—MATTHEW 12:47

"I understand my son can't see me right now," Mary said
knowingly to the apostle. "I'm sure he's running into
opposition." The apostle concurred. "Jesus just told us that
God's reign suffers violence and the violent are taking it by
force. Yesterday he reproached several towns for lacking any
repentance. Mary, he's being attacked constantly, not just
when we picked grain on the Sabbath, but when Pharisees
accused him of using demonic power to work miracles." Mary
gasped. "I can't believe it. I knew Israel's leaders were tough,
but this? My son needs me to go to prayer," she finished, taking
the arms of Jesus' two cousins. "Give him this bread with our
love," she told the apostle. "He has important work to do. I'll
talk to him later. He always makes time for his mother."

Micah 7:14–15,18–20
Psalm 85:2–4,5–6,7–8
Matthew 12:46–50

Say not, "I am too young."
To whomever I send you, you shall go;
whatever I command you, you shall speak."
—JEREMIAH 1:7

Right now, where you live, someone needs you to speak a word of truth and to do something to uphold justice. It's a work in your house, neighborhood, family, or jobsite that no one but you can do. Your baptismal call as priest, prophet, and king demands action today. We all have legit excuses: "I'm tired. I did good yesterday. I'm too old. Let someone else walk in that march, serve at that food bank, help the migrants and refugees." Sorry, that doesn't cut it, Jeremiah cajoles. "Get serious. Be prophetic. No excuses." Take a page from God's pep talk to Jeremiah and take risks. Have no fear. God is recruiting you.

Jeremiah 1:1,4–10
Psalm 71:1–2,3–4a,5–6ab,15 and 17
Matthew 13:1–9

Thursday

JULY 21

• ST. LAWRENCE OF BRINDISI, PRIEST AND DOCTOR OF THE CHURCH •

*[Jesus said,] "They look but do not see and hear but do not listen
or understand."*
—MATTHEW 13:13

The car screeched to a stop. The little boy picked up his ball,
oblivious to mortal danger. His dad, watching, couldn't move
fast enough. He shuddered in sheer horror as he scooped up
his only child. He'd told him a thousand times never to run
into the street. But his son covered his ears, kicked, and
pushed dad away until the father allowed the boy to descend.
The son has no idea how precious and fragile his life is and
how many choices may lead him astray as he grows. When
will he learn? (This is God and us.)

Jeremiah 2:1–3,7–8,12–13
Psalm 36:6–7ab,8–9,10–11
Matthew 13:10–17

Friday

JULY 22

• ST. MARY MAGDALENE •

Jesus said to her, "Woman, why are you weeping?
Whom are you looking for?"
—JOHN 20:13

In 2016 Pope Francis elevated to a feast the celebration of
this apostle to the apostles. In today's Gospel, St. Mary waits
at the tomb after two apostles came and went. She grieves
and wonders. She stays. What would've happened had the
two apostles stayed? Courageously, St. Mary dares to bend
down and look into the grave. Angels speak to her. Is Gabriel
making an appearance again? Tears of desolation obstruct her
eyesight as the voice asks who she's looking for. It is a
defining moment. She encounters the risen Jesus. She will
tell this story thousands of times after this. Wouldn't you? A
first-person, with-her-own-eyes witness, St. Mary will forever
remember the sights, smells, and touch of that morning
turned into an unforgettable consolation.

MEMORIAL
Song of Songs 3:1–4b or 2 Corinthians 5:14–17
Psalm 63:2,3–4,5–6,8–9
John 20:1–2,11–18

Saturday

JULY 23

• ST. BRIDGET OF SWEDEN, RELIGIOUS •

Stand at the gate of the house of the LORD. . . .
—JEREMIAH 7:2

When you picture God's residence, what do you imagine? Palaces, clouds, and thrones? Or your own heart? You are God's special, chosen dwelling place! How wonderful are you! Of all the houses the Lord could have chosen, God wants the human heart. Not only that, but God's throne room? Yes, it's your mouth, the place where Eucharist arrives. How beautiful/handsome is your mouth, your smile, your words! And even when they are sullied, God arrives anyway, taking up residence in the cave of your mouth and then your body, despite your failings. This passage uses the exclamation point to proclaim how spiritually good-looking you are in God's eyes. Take several moments to marvel at the lovely dwelling place of God: you. Oh. And the people next door. And those who disagree with or hurt you.

Jeremiah 7:1–11
Psalm 84:3,4,5–6a and 8a,11
Matthew 13:24–30

Sunday

JULY 24

• SEVENTEENTH SUNDAY IN ORDINARY TIME •

He will get up to give him whatever he needs
because of his persistence.
—LUKE 11:8

Jesus invites me to ask with the expectation that I will
receive. Sometimes my requests seem pretty impossible to
fill, and I find myself apologizing even before asking. "This is
a lot to ask, God, but. . . ." Yet I believe that God cares
deeply, better than any friend, about even the smallest
things. God probably loves microbes and molecules. Will I
learn something about myself by asking repeatedly? When I
hear myself say something out loud, I hear it in a new way. Is
that why God wants me to ask persistently? What will I learn
about myself by asking again? Will I compose a new reason
why I think my request deserves a yes?

Genesis 18:20–32
Psalm 138:1–2,2–3,6–7,7–8 (3a)
Colossians 2:12–14
Luke 11:1–13

Monday

JULY 25

• ST. JAMES, APOSTLE •

[Jesus said,] "Whoever wishes to be great among you
shall be your servant."
—MATTHEW 20:26

Their mother speaks: "I missed the parable Jesus told about a
landowner paying equal wages to someone who worked
eight hours and another who worked one. Had I heard that,
plus Jesus' prediction about crucifixion, I wouldn't have
requested leadership positions for my sons. It seemed like a
good idea at the time, but the reign of God is apparently
nothing like I expected. For one, it isn't fair. Jesus' leaders
won't get specially trimmed outfits or all-expenses-paid
lifestyles. Jesus is a radical. My husband had to hire extra
hands now that our boys follow Jesus. Was it wrong of me to
want recognition for their sacrifices? The reign of God is
demanding the absolute best from me: the lives of my
precious sons."

2 Corinthians 4:7–15
Psalm 126:1bc–2ab,2cd–3,4–5,6
Matthew 20:20–28

Tuesday

JULY 26

The field is the world, the good seed
the children of the Kingdom.
The weeds are the children of the Evil One.
—MATTHEW 13:38

Consider Jesus the sower described today. He liberally sprinkles us across the plain, knowing the soil is good, and we will have what we need to grow into the harvest he wants to collect. On the far side of the field, the mortal enemy of humanity sows discord, suspicion, fear, and every kind of malice. The wind blows and the seeds intermingle, planting themselves amidst one another. As the rain falls, evil tries to choke out the good plants. Fear not. God tends and prunes, preparing for an abundant yield.

Jeremiah 14:17–22
Psalm 79:8,9,11 and 13
Matthew 13:36–43

Wednesday

JULY 27

*[Jesus said,] "The kingdom of heaven is like a treasure
buried in a field."*
—MATTHEW 13:44

To what can we compare the reign of God in our own day? It
is like a single email that goes viral within a minute, or a
social media post that acquires five million likes. What
electronic words might further God's message of love for all
people? Do you want the world to be a little bit better
because you were here? What will you post to social media
today? Send a word of encouraging love and wait for God to
give the increase. Someone who will connect electronically
needs love and courage today. Buried in all your electronic
communications, look for a pearl to share.

Jeremiah 15:10,16–21
Psalm 59:2–3,4,10–11,17,18
Matthew 13:44–46

Thursday

JULY 28

Indeed, like clay in the hand of the potter,
so are you in my hand, house of Israel.
—JEREMIAH 18:6

Remember the song "He's Got the Whole World in His Hands"? Imagine the Creator rolling the clay of the earth between two enormous palms, rubbing infinite possibilities and gifts into every aspect of the globe. Then this divine Artist breathes the atmosphere into being, pronouncing it very good. But humanity carelessly overheats this home and ignores science's warnings for too long. Dearest Potter, please breathe on your creation again to heal our atmosphere. We have sinned against your creation, wasting resources that belonged to future generations. Oh, capable Artist, you can fix this! Push us back into shape that we might again follow your lead and care for planet Earth.

Jeremiah 18:1–6
Psalm 146:1b–2,3–4,5–6ab
Matthew 13:47–53

Friday

JULY 29

• ST. MARTHA, ST. MARY, AND ST. LAZARUS •

Beloved, let us love one another, because love is of God; everyone who loves is begotten of God and knows God.
—1 JOHN 4:7

First, we are loved. It's that experience that draws us into faith. Only from there can we go on to be loving. And in so doing, we participate in God. Julian of Norwich came to understand that all that is made is sustained and held in existence by the love of God. God begets love. And without love, the world grinds to a halt. Love folds onto love and returns to where it began: with God. It follows, therefore, that anyone who loves is participating in God-ness. Whether they realize it or not, God is at work within them. God will recognize God's self when that person arrives at their demise. Welcome home, beloved lover.

MEMORIAL
1 John 4:7-16
Psalm 34: 2–3,4–5, 6–7,8–9,10–11
John 11:19–27 or Luke 10:38–42

I am afflicted and in pain;
let your saving help, O God, protect me.
I will praise the name of God in song.
—PSALM 69:30–31A

Quagmire. Quicksand. Discouragement. But the psalmist doesn't give up. Despite an abyss threatening to swallow her up, the soul praises God. Have you tried this when you are down? A flood of emotions can overwhelm the soul to the point where it feels in desperate need of reviving. How can this be accomplished? Through praise. It pulls the soul out of the morass of sinking thoughts. Expect God to offer assistance. We are dependent on God, not the other way around. It may take affliction to make us notice this. Patience. Don't make any hasty changes. Turn from the bog and into praising God, who never gives up on anyone.

Jeremiah 26:11–16,24
Psalm 69:15–16,30–31,33–34
Matthew 14:1–12

Sunday
JULY 31

• EIGHTEENTH SUNDAY IN ORDINARY TIME •

Vanity of vanities! All things are vanity!
—ECCLESIASTES 1:2B

St. Ignatius, who died on July 31, 1556, owes his conversion to a cannonball. He was once so full of vanity that he had his leg rebroken in the hope of looking good in fashionable tights at court. Teenage dreams of soldiering dissolved into serving Divine Majesty in the battle for souls. God can use anything to attract humanity, even war wounds. As patron saint of soldiers, St. Ignatius chose to bear Christ's standard (flag) and synthesized many tools into the *Spiritual Exercises*, a retreat still popular after five hundred years. It's a reason he is patron saint of retreats, too. Have you made a retreat lately? May we turn from vain pursuits to praise and reverence and serve God our Lord, and be saved by doing this.

Ecclesiastes 1:2; 2:21–23
Psalm 90:3–4,5–6,12–13,14,17 (1)
Colossians 3:1–5,9–11
Luke 12:13–21

Monday

AUGUST 1

Sinners wait to destroy me,
but I pay heed to your decrees.
—PSALM 119:95

This psalm might foreshadow the end of Jesus' temptations in the desert, when the evil spirit leaves Jesus to wait for another opportunity. When life's pace is hectic, it's especially important to pay attention, because it's easier to miss the insidious infiltration of the serpent. Suddenly a primrose path beckons, but it soon turns to desolation. Jesus knew how to pay heed to his path. After all, he is the Way. And he paid great attention to religious leaders trying to destroy him, hoping for their conversion. Even when sinners plot destruction, be confident that God's decree of love always wins.

Jeremiah 28:1–17
Psalm 119:29,43,79,80,95,102
Matthew 14:13–21

Tuesday

AUGUST 2

Jesus made the disciples get into the boat
and precede him to the other side of the sea,
while he dismissed the crowds.
—MATTHEW 14:22

I knew Jesus wanted to be alone, even before the crowd appeared. News of his cousin John's death hit him hard. I wished I could ease his grief, but he asked me to get in the boat, so I did. It didn't make sense to me, but I joined the others. What if enemies came for him? What if we got lost? "I'll find you," he said with a comforting tone. Still, I didn't like seeing his figure grow smaller as he ministered to the stragglers on the beach. Putting his needs second all day, Jesus healed, taught, and fed. And now he listened, nodded, and hugged. I don't know where he finds the strength.

Jeremiah 30:1–2,12–15,18–22
Psalm 102:16–18,19–21,29 and 22–23
Matthew 14:22–36 or 15:1–2,10–14

"Have pity on me, Lord, Son of David!"
—MATTHEW 15:22

Baby Grace struggled for life. "Please pray," a dear one asked. I was not above begging. "God, have mercy! I can only imagine her parents' heartbreak; please let her live. Breath of God, breathe into her." I prayed with desperation, knowing that not all prayers are answered the way I hope they will be. The Canaanite woman was not above begging on behalf of her daughter either. She was a real person, and I believe she's in heaven with Jesus. I asked her to join us in interceding for this newborn. Why should Jesus listen to us? Because with age-old love, God loves and keeps mercy toward Israel, which includes us. Five months later, I received a picture of Grace in her mother's arms, coming home from the hospital for the first time.

Jeremiah 31:1–7
Jeremiah 31:10,11–12ab,13
Matthew 15:21–28

Thursday

AUGUST 4

• ST. JOHN MARY VIANNEY, PRIEST •

[Jesus said,] "But who do you say that I am?"
—MATTHEW 16:15

Jesus, fully human, experienced the usual desires, including the hope of being heard and understood. "Am I getting through to these people?" he may have wondered. "How much of my message are they internalizing? Are they understanding that Jeremiah predicted the very covenant I come to establish? Oh! If they only knew how deeply they are loved!" How painful it must have been for Jesus to hear Pharisees say, "Who do you think you are?" And how refreshing for Jesus to receive confirmation through Peter's words that he was heard in some fashion. In our spiritual walk, we often seek confirmation for the path we are choosing. Jesus was consoled, and perhaps filled with joy, knowing that Peter was receiving revelation from the heavenly Father.

Jeremiah 31:31–34
Psalm 51:12–13,14–15,18–19
Matthew 16:13–23

Friday

AUGUST 5

See, upon the mountains there advances
the bearer of good news,
announcing peace!
—NAHUM 2:1

On the Esquiline Hill in Rome in the fourth century, snow miraculously fell in August, beginning the devotion to Our Lady of the Snows. A childless couple had prayed for a sign. They wanted to place their fortune at God's disposal through the intercession of Mary. How best to do it? It is said that snow fell in the shape of the basilica's footprint. This largest of Marian churches in Rome is said to contain the crib of Jesus. Four basilicas and three churches comprise a pilgrimage for those who cannot visit the Holy Land. One of the stops includes a piece of what St. Helena identified as Christ's cross.

Nahum 2:1,3; 3:1–3,6–7
Deuteronomy 32:35cd–36ab,39abcd,41
Matthew 16:24–28

We had been eyewitnesses of his majesty.
For he received honor and glory from God the Father.
—2 PETER 1:16–17

What would it be like months later to retell the experience of seeing Jesus aglow with divine light and hearing God's voice? Jesus knew his friends would need time to process the revelation. "Don't talk about it just yet," he asked. The transfiguration would change *them*. Much later Peter would use what he saw as further proof to listeners that Jesus is God's Son and our Savior. "We didn't make this up. We heard God while hiking with Jesus." Every believer gets invitations to mountaintop experiences, but not everyone pays attention, pauses, or says yes to a risky path. It costs to leave comfortable situations, to take steep, arduous paths, and have no guarantee of success, a theophany, or consolations.

Daniel 7:9–10,13–14
Psalm 97:1–2,5–6,9
2 Peter 1:16–19
Luke 9:28b–36

Sell your belongings and give alms.
Provide money bags for yourselves that do not wear out.
—LUKE 12:33

The descendants of Joseph in Egypt knew about the Passover
in advance so that they might develop the courage to head to
the desert, the Wisdom reading today explains. If eating the
lamb kept them safe from the death of their firstborn loved
ones, how much more could they rely on and follow God
anywhere, leaving their belongings behind? The meal
strengthened their faith and resolve. "Don't be afraid, little
flock," Jesus says in the Gospel. Are we ready to head to the
desert of self-sacrificing service? If our ancestors could live in
tents, waiting for God to make the foundations of their new
nation, can we give up personal comfort and exercise the grit
and determination required to follow Christ?

Wisdom 18:6–9
Psalm 33:1,12,18–19,20–22 (12b)
Hebrews 11:1–2,8–19 or 11:1–2, 8–12
Luke 12:32–48

Monday

AUGUST 8

• ST. DOMINIC, PRIEST •

And they were overwhelmed with grief.
—MATTHEW 17:23

Hearing the whole message in a conversation can be tough. Jesus' sentence about being killed was so shocking that the disciples couldn't listen to the next part. What an emotional roller coaster to follow Jesus. One day it's miracles and healings. The next he says he'll be killed after being handed over to enemies. No wonder they were overwhelmed! Have you experienced a showstopper comment in a conversation that causes you to say, "Wait. Back up. I can't hear any more. I need those words to sink in. You said *what?*" Clarifying questions precede moving ahead. The statement will make more sense in hindsight or after further reflection.

Ezekiel 1:2–5,24–28c
Psalm 148:1–2,11–12,13,14
Matthew 17:22–27

How sweet to my palate are your promises,
sweeter than honey to my mouth!
—PSALM 119:103

Poetry is often cryptic; psalms written centuries before Christ carry some difficult-to-discern metaphors. Perhaps this one foreshadows Holy Communion. The promise of Christ's return, confirmed by his eucharistic presence, causes sweetness in our souls. Christ enters his chosen throne room: our mouths. Pause before swallowing, knowing what a poor reception we loved sinners have to offer God. Savor, like the first bite of a favorite food. Experience a tangy sensation when taste buds react to a new flavor. Jesus is a strong sweetness. Allow your palate to be overwhelmed with humility and love.

Ezekiel 2:8—3:4
Psalm 119:14,24,72,103,111,131
Matthew 18:1–5,10,12–14

Whoever sows sparingly will also reap sparingly,
and whoever sows bountifully
will also reap bountifully.
—2 CORINTHIANS 9:6

Tony the cashier watched her enter the store and pause again
at the artificial tree, as she had the week before. Now 80
percent off, it attracted her, but on her fixed income, Fran
couldn't justify spending $3.99. She deliberated and finally
decided to splurge. Before ringing her up, Tony dug through
his wallet and pulled out his last five-dollar bill. He used it to
pay for the tree. Fran was flabbergasted. "Nobody's ever done
anything like that for me before!" she said. She'd seen his
near-empty wallet and knew from his attire that he also
struggled. When he handed her the change, she pocketed it
in amazement, not realizing the additional gift until she was
outside. God loves a cheerful giver.

2 Corinthians 9:6–10
Psalm 112:1–2,5–6,7–8,9
John 12:24–26

Thursday

AUGUST 11

• ST. CLARE, VIRGIN •

They angered him with their high places
and with their idols roused his jealousy.
—PSALM 78:58

When St. Clare followed the example of St. Francis of Assisi,
she renounced wealth and status. While her family at first
was angry, her widowed mother eventually joined Clare in
the Poor Ladies, later named the Poor Clares. Their convent
in Assisi stands on a high place different from those
referenced in today's psalm; the lush valley spread below is a
vivid reminder of the expansive goodness of God. No idol of
materialism stands there. At the stone fountain in front of the
Poor Clare's edifice, simplicity rules. In a silent and plain
chapel is the cross that spoke to St. Francis, asking him to
rebuild the church. Pilgrims learn that the works of the Most
High are not easily forgotten there.

Ezekiel 12:1–12
Psalm 78:56–57,58–59,61–62
Matthew 18:21—19:1

Friday

AUGUST 12

*Yet I will remember the covenant I made with
you when you were a girl,
and I will set up an everlasting covenant with you.*
—EZEKIEL 16:60

Do you ever feel that you are wallowing in the mess you
made? Ezekiel reminds Israel of its sinful condition. When
you fall again into an old pattern of habitual sin, it can be
tempting to feel discouraged. Get up! God is still calling you!
Even if you feel like a zombie bride rather than a spotless
virgin, God is indeed your savior. Courage! So you feel
ashamed and you have no excuses. God still pardons all you
have done. Yes, all. Like a loving mother, God can scrub you
up and make you good as new, wrap you in a fluffy towel,
and cradle you in loving, forgiving arms. Remember your
baptism! Start fresh.

Ezekiel 16:1–15,60,63 or 16:59–63
Isaiah 12:2–3,4bcd,5–6
Matthew 19:3–12

[Jesus said,] "Let the children come to me, and do not
prevent them."
—MATTHEW 19:14

I wanted to show Jesus my rock, shaped like a heart! It's really cool. He smiled, and I knew I was loved. So I gave him my prized possession because I loved him back. "We have important work to do," a grown-up said. I felt hurt, but it didn't last. Jesus squatted to my level and said, "I see a heart in the rock, too. Look how nicely it fits in my hand. I will keep it and take it with me on my journey until I find another child who needs a gift of a new heart." I stood a little taller. And yet I felt sad. "Don't go!" I said. He smiled, pointed to my chest, and said, "Don't worry. I will always be *right here*."

Ezekiel 18:1–10,13b,30–32
Psalm 51:12–13,14–15,18–19
Matthew 19:13–15

Since we are surrounded by so great a cloud of witnesses,
let us rid ourselves of every burden and sin
that clings to us
and persevere in running the race.
—HEBREWS 12:1

The stadium is packed with cheering fans as I come around the
track for the next lap. I look up and see Thérèse of Lisieux
jumping up and down. There's Vincent de Paul waving a
banner wildly. I see Anne, Jesus' grandma, shouting, "You got
this! Keep going!" They all watch and root for me. I sweat and
strain, wondering if I have the strength to complete the race. I
drop a backpack of sin, and the crowd leaps to its feet. Jesus,
teach me endurance, just like you had in moving through the
Crucifixion. You knew joy lay ahead—that we'd be together in
heaven. A victor's crown awaits.

Jeremiah 38:4–6,8–10
Psalm 40:2,3,4,18 (14b)
Hebrews 12:1–4
Luke 12:49–53

Monday

AUGUST 15

• THE ASSUMPTION OF THE BLESSED VIRGIN MARY •

The woman herself fled into the desert
where she had a place prepared by God.
—REVELATION 12:6

She wailed. She suffered. She labored in pain. And all her
selfless mothering produced a son strong and caring. He
knew so much because of her. She ran frequently into the
desert of prayer, demonstrating to her only son the
importance of praying first and then acting. No one should
have to suffer the loss of a child, whatever age. But she did,
and God reached a hand to her and welcomed her into a safe
home readied for her at the beginning of time. All of heaven
rejoiced as the female Ark of the Covenant was lifted up to
shouts of joy, just as crowds played raucous music while
David danced before the tent.

Revelation 11:19a; 12:1–6a,10ab
Psalm 45:10,11,12,16
1 Corinthians 15:20–27
Luke 1:39–56

Tuesday

AUGUST 16

• ST. STEPHEN OF HUNGARY •

[Jesus said,] "Amen, I say to you, it will be hard for one who is rich
to enter the Kingdom of heaven."
—MATTHEW 19:23

It's difficult to embrace poverty in a culture where people
have so much stuff. Most houses don't seem to have enough
closet space, and quick storage facilities pop up everywhere.
What does it feel like to give something to someone who
needs it? Perhaps it's easy to loan a lawn mower or offer spare
garage space to someone in need of temporary storage space.
A first step might be praying for the grace to even *want* to be
rid of possessions.

Ezekiel 28:1–10
Deuteronomy 32:26–27ab,27cd–28,30,35cd–36ab
Matthew 19:23–30

AUGUST 17

He guides me in right paths
for his name's sake.
—PSALM 23:3

The shepherd watched his silly sheep bumping into one
another and walking aimlessly about. They really were quite
adorable even though they weren't all that smart. When he
realized one had strayed, he chuckled. "Isn't that just like my
sheep," he thought. "I love them, but they really don't know
themselves as well as I know them. And look. There he is:
caught in those same thorn bushes I've taken him out of so
many times before. Perhaps this time he'll realize that the
bush is trouble and will stop going there. I'll watch him a
little longer, hoping he learns his lesson. It's good for him to
struggle, because he'll learn from that, even though his
memory is so short." The shepherd stifled a loving laugh and
rescued his darling again.

Ezekiel 34:1–11
Psalm 23:1–3a,3b–4,5,6
Matthew 20:1–16

AUGUST 18

"Everything is ready; come to the feast."
—MATTHEW 22:4

It's heartbreaking how many times God tells us how favored we are and then gets rejected. For generations the message has been the same: "I want you. I desire you. Choose me! I'm your God." And how crushing when people we love ignore, discount, or disbelieve this unrequited Lover. How can this be? "As soon as I get through grad school . . . this work project . . . this family crisis . . . this accumulation of a nest egg . . . then I can look into this God thing." But the feast is waiting. Imagine that going to Mass is like Sunday dinner planned by your favorite grandma. She set the table with her best dishes, made all your favorite foods, even wrapped presents for you, and waited. And you never showed. God waits for us every week, hoping we'll share the greatest meal ever prepared.

Ezekiel 36:23–28
Psalm 51:12–13,14–15,18–19
Matthew 22:1–14

Friday

AUGUST 19

• ST. JOHN EUDES, PRIEST •

*O my people, I will open your graves
and have you rise from them.*
—EZEKIEL 37:12

At Mass today the priest offered the sign of peace and emphasized an important word: "The peace of the *risen* Lord be with you!" The priest said it with such genuine enthusiasm that I looked over my shoulder to see if Jesus was standing there. He was, in the face of a parishioner. The risen Lord is all around on this August day. Resurrection is the exciting truth that we have a joyful hope in a future full of love. It's no empty pledge, nor is it new. Ezekiel foretold it. Did his listeners yawn as people sometimes do when the homily disappoints? Peace is a grace that God is eager to give. Peace and resurrection: believe in them.

Ezekiel 37:1–14
Psalm 107:2–3,4–5,6–7,8–9
Matthew 22:34–40

The greatest among you must be your servant.
—MATTHEW 23:11

In the twelfth century, St. Bernard talked so persuasively that people joined monasteries, started crusades, and ended a schism in Rome. He lived from a very full heart. When at age twenty he joined a monastic community, so did thirty friends and several relatives. Think about what you were doing (or hope to do) at that age. Consider whether you have ever spoken so convincingly that someone changed their view. Jesus uses the analogy of trees bearing fruit to highlight how words yield storerooms full of goodness. Take a moment to review your words thus far this day. They are a product of your heart; words say volumes about your thoughts, mood, and inner inclinations. Thank God for what you observe, because God works through all things.

Ezekiel 43:1–7ab
Psalm 85:9ab and 10, 11–12,13–14
Matthew 23:1–12

[Jesus said,] "For behold, some are last who will be first,
and some are first who will be last."
—LUKE 13:30

If we needed another motivating factor to serve people who
are poor, Jesus' instructions about who will enter heaven
ought to get us moving. We can do something for a world
damaged in multiple ways. We know how to make clean
water available, for example, but the World Health
Organization estimates that by 2025, more than half of the
people in the world will be living in water-stressed areas.
Nearly one in ten people in the world (about 600 million
people) die preventable deaths after eating contaminated
food *every year*. Are we putting ourselves first while people
wail and suffer needlessly right now in this world? God's
reign rewards those who put themselves last.

Isaiah 66:18–21
Psalm 117:1,2
Hebrews 12:5–7,11–13
Luke 13:22–30

Monday

AUGUST 22

• THE QUEENSHIP OF THE BLESSED VIRGIN MARY •

His dominion is vast
and forever peaceful,
From David's throne, and over his kingdom,
which he confirms and sustains
By judgment and justice,
both now and forever.
—ISAIAH 9:6

Did Mary know on her deathbed that from then on people across the ages would call her a queen? Mary said yes to Gabriel, and her *Magnificat* confirmed her realization that she would be blessed for all time. When her Son, the King, entered Jerusalem on a donkey, a sign of peace and nonviolence, did Mary witness it and understand? When she saw Jesus crucified, did she understand more fully what being a queen in the kingdom of God would mean?

MEMORIAL
Isaiah 9:1–6
Psalm 113:1–2,3–4,5–6,7–8
Luke 1:26–38; Matthew 23:13–22

[Jesus said,] "Woe to you, scribes and Pharisees, you hypocrites."
—MATTHEW 23:23

Marvin was wading in minutiae while important tasks in his life remained undone. Distractions were one problem, but he also focused on someone else's disagreeable opinion, political stance, and behaviors worthy of criticism. He didn't mean to judge, but he sure did. It kept him from looking at his own shortcomings. After praying, he related to the Pharisees. He realized he had been offering himself excuses. No matter what, God loves, and when Marvin discovered he was acting like a Pharisee described in Scripture, he turned to Jesus. That's all it took. He received forgiveness.

2 Thessalonians 2:1–3a,14–17
Psalm 96:10,11–12,13
Matthew 23:23–26

Jesus answered and said to [Nathanael],
"Do you believe
because I told you that I saw you under the fig tree?
You will see greater things than this."
—JOHN 1:50

Jesus laughed out loud! Oh, sure, John used the words "answered and said," but he did that to avoid embarrassing me, Nathanael. Jesus laughed when I expressed astonishment after learning that he saw me under the fig tree. Only God could've known what I was thinking as I sat there. I was praying for the grace to be able to meet the Messiah! Pretty arrogant of me. When my friend Philip ran up to tell me he'd found the Messiah, it seemed too big a coincidence. I'm not usually skeptical, but Nazareth? Really? But when Jesus spoke, he touched my gut with an authenticity and omniscience I couldn't deny. Jesus, you had me at "fig tree."

Revelation 21:9b–14
Psalm 145:10–11,12–13,17–18
John 1:45–51

[Jesus said,] "Stay awake!
For you do not know on which day your Lord will come."
—MATTHEW 24:42

You don't get the whole month. Well, you might, but you never know. You can be tempted to plan and prepare and be ready for every event, appointment, and occasion for the coming year. But your life may be required of you this very night. Live today, join God in expressing love , and listen for the Master's invitations to serve. Cherish this unrepeatable minute. Spend today reverencing God. If you were to die tomorrow, what would you want to do today? Do that.

1 Corinthians 1:1–9
Psalm 145:2–3,4–5,6–7
Matthew 24:42–51

Friday

AUGUST 26

The LORD brings to nought the plans of nations;
he foils the designs of peoples.
But the plan of the LORD stands forever;
the design of his heart, through all generations.
—PSALM 33:10–11

God looks down on all creation, aware of every heart immediately. With just a word, God made wondrous galaxies and miniscule atoms. The nature of God inspires awe, which is sometimes translated as fear. It's the kind of overwhelming emotion evoked when looking down into the Colorado River from the world's highest concrete arch bridge. Hoover Dam below looks small. People naturally gasp and step back from the bridge's edge. That's nothing compared to God's power.

Humanity forgets this. Leaders strategize as if they can control tomorrow. They can't. And even if they could, it wouldn't turn out as great as the future God already planned and holds in mind.

1 Corinthians 1:17–25
Psalm 33:1–2,4–5,10–11
Matthew 25:1–13

Saturday

AUGUST 27

• ST. MONICA •

"Master, you gave me five talents."
—MATTHEW 25:20

Each person has special talents. Perhaps they come to mind immediately; perhaps not. Something difficult for one is easy for another. One way to identify your talents is to notice what you love to do. God put deep within each person a joy that can be discovered when expressing a special talent. It could be artistic, culinary, interpersonal, or something else. Ask God to reveal what talents you have that you may not be fully using. Find some silence and listen for clues. They say St. Monica had a talent for nagging her son about his poor choices. She even nagged God, praying incessantly for St. Augustine's conversion. It worked. How will you exercise a special talent today and do one thing to make yourself smile?

1 Corinthians 1:26–31
Psalm 33:12–13,18–19,20–21
Matthew 25:14–30

AUGUST 28

• TWENTY-SECOND SUNDAY IN ORDINARY TIME •

Humble yourself the more, the greater you are,
and you will find favor with God.
—SIRACH 3:18

People don't seem to be lining up at the Humility Outlet.
The Pride Store is much more popular. They always run
two-for-one sales. God is the proprietor at the Humility
Outlet, and the cashier sure looks like Jesus, who, though he
was divine, did not seek equality with God. In fact, pride in
knowing he was the Messiah was a temptation, not only in
the desert after his baptism. St. Ignatius writes about three
ways of being humble, the third of which is to be a person
who desires poverty. Not everyone is called to this third way,
which is a God-given grace. But at the very back of the
Humility Outlet, you will find a door to the Poverty Market.

Sirach 3:17–18,20,28–29
Psalm 68:4–5,6–7,10–11
Hebrews 12:18–19,22–24a
Luke 14:1,7–14

———————————

The king was deeply distressed,
but because of his oaths and the guests,
he did not wish to break his word.
—MARK 6:26

On the surface, it seems like a good goal: not breaking one's word. But evil disguises itself. The greater good would be to break a foolish promise rather than to commit a murder. And really, this is about the king's reputation and desire to look powerful and resolute in front of peers. You would never make a bad choice to impress *your* friends, would you? If you listened to a distasteful conversation at a business dinner and said nothing, not wanting to be the center of attention, you may have felt distressed for not speaking up. While hoping to blend into the wallpaper, you may have allowed vile words to stand unchecked. Father, forgive!

1 Corinthians 2:1–5
Psalm 119:97,98,99,100,101,102
Mark 6:17–29

AUGUST 30

"What is there about his word?
For with authority and power he commands
the unclean spirits,
and they come out."
—LUKE 4:36B

God is a verb. Creator creating. Love loving. Savior saving.
God never stops working on creation, and we, humble
humans, are invited to cocreate. God implants some
astonishing words inside us. *Hope. Service. Forgiveness.* What is
there about our words today that will inspire others to love
with the love that God is? God is not inaction. God loves
laboring with us. We think too small and expect too little; we
could be accomplishing more miracles if we let Jesus work
through us, through faith. As beloved children we have God,
Jesus the Word, alive in us.

1 Corinthians 2:10b–16
Psalm 145:8–9,10–11,12–13ab,13cd–14
Luke 4:31–37

AUGUST 31

For we are God's co-workers;
you are God's field, God's building.
—1 CORINTHIANS 3:9

People go in and out of skyscrapers, never really thinking about the minds that devised everything from elevators to infrastructure. The wiring guy knows nothing of the interior decorator. People take for granted that the building is sound.

Colleagues collaborate side by side, keeping in mind the goals of a project. It doesn't matter which person comes up with the great idea or the perfect solution to the roadblock. What's important is the final product. The building of God's reign involves not competition but cooperation. If beliefs differ slightly or someone has only a part of the story, that's not as important as the common ground and the love of God being spread to every human heart. God constantly is at work in people's lives, often in the background or subconsciously. God beckons us gently.

1 Corinthians 3:1–9
Psalm 33:12–13,14–15,20–21
Luke 4:38–44

SEPTEMBER 1

*"Put out in the deep water and lower your nets" . . . When they had done
this, they caught a great number of fish.*
—LUKE 5:4,6

Like many people, I own a home with two large yards and all
that fills them. Or do I? The avocado seed I planted out back
is now a tree twice my height, but no fruit yet. Someday
when we sell this house, the new owners will enjoy its
avocados. I thank God for the lemons off a tree that others
planted, oranges from neighbors, and kale from a friend.
Growing up, I thought food came from stores. The earth is
full of growth I cannot control. God makes it happen. Let's
thank God for it. Plants full of nutritious vitamins keep us
alive. God, the great initiator, allows us to live. In reality, we
own nothing but the free choices we make. Let's choose God
in all things.

1 Corinthians 3:18–23
Psalm 24:1bc–2,3–4ab,5–6
Luke 5:1–11

*It does not concern me in the least
that I be judged by you or any human tribunal;
I do not even pass judgment on myself.*
—1 CORINTHIANS 4:3

What an attitude! Paul holds up quite an example; his advice
is even more timely today than when his community argued
about circumcision. How can church members be channels
of peace instead of instruments of disapproval? We all have
sinned, but we pick out someone else's faults and judge them
while ignoring our own failings and sins. The world needs
more love than criticism. Of course, it's normal human
development for young people to stress about peer pressure.
Age brings wisdom that is less concerned about the opinions
of others. Let Jesus be the judge.

1 Corinthians 4:1–5
Psalm 37:3–4,5–6,27–28,39–40
Luke 5:33–39

Saturday

SEPTEMBER 3

• ST. GREGORY THE GREAT, POPE AND DOCTOR OF THE CHURCH •

When ridiculed, we bless; when persecuted, we endure;
when slandered, we respond gently.
—1 CORINTHIANS 4:12–13

It's always a good idea to assume that people mean well. *Did I hear that right?* is a better thought than, *He's crazy.* Be eager to put a positive interpretation on another's remarks, hoping that their intention is good. Ask for clarification when hearing something unfavorable rather than slam an angry mental door and walk away. Further, if unable to interpret it favorably, or when negativity is confirmed, it's better to correct the person with love. Good communication is essential. Ask God for the grace of gratitude, which serves as medicine against slander, crude speech, and other bad responses.

1 Corinthians 4:6b–15
Psalm 145:17–18,19–20,21
Luke 6:1–5

SEPTEMBER 4

• TWENTY-THIRD SUNDAY IN ORDINARY TIME •

*Who can know God's counsel,
or who can conceive what the LORD intends?*
—WISDOM 9:13

We need you down here, Abba! Can't you see what we're
going through? What are you thinking to allow this mess to
continue? We expected you to intervene and stop this
madness long ago. And yet here we are. We think we've done
our part; we planned and measured, set up expectations, and
considered the costs. *Kablooey!* We witness a natural disaster,
we suffer through illness, or we watch our dreams
disintegrate. How can anything good result from this latest
calamity! Yet we believe you constantly infuse your Holy
Spirit into humanity. Once again we renounce sin and all its
empty promises. Please make your plans known to us. We
know that, coming from you, they are for the good.

Wisdom 9:13–18b
Psalm 90:3–4,5–6,12–13,14 and 17 (1)
Philemon 9–10,12–17
Luke 14:25–33

SEPTEMBER 5

*Do you not know that a little yeast leavens
all the dough?*
—1 CORINTHIANS 5:6

He had a jar in the refrigerator with what looked like slimy yellowed milk. It was ugly. A close friend visiting offered to throw out what appeared to be forgotten leftovers. "No! It's my sourdough bread starter!" It had a long history and a story attached. He'd received it from a special person, who received it from . . . you get the idea. It was a valued chain of relationships. Sometimes that little bit of yeast that infects a whole batch of dough isn't pretty. But the fragrance of fresh-baked bread in the house is amazing. Yeast can be compared to the reign of God, but it's also an analogy for one poor choice leading to a bad habit. Soon it can become a lifestyle that poisons my relationship with God.

1 Corinthians 5:1–8
Psalm 5:5–6,7,12
Luke 6:6–11

SEPTEMBER 6

*And he came down with them and stood
on a stretch of level ground.*
—LUKE 6:17

Jesus leaves his prayer to come among his followers. God
comes down to be with you, too. Jesus—this man who is
God—has never left you. Jesus didn't operate in isolation. In
this Gospel he starts with an all-nighter of prayer. Have you
ever done that? An hour seems possible, but all night? Jesus
comes down to whatever low point you have this month.
Jesus gets down on his knees to look you in the eye. Jesus
takes your hands and lifts you up. He pulls you to your feet
and stands with you. He makes the ground level for you.

1 Corinthians 6:1–11
Psalm 149:1b–2,3–4,5–6a and 9b
Luke 6:12–19

⇒ 283 ⇐

SEPTEMBER 7

Blessed are you when people hate you,
and when they exclude and insult you,
and denounce your name as evil
on account of the Son of Man.
Rejoice and leap for joy on that day!
—LUKE 6:22–23

The strength of my convictions led me to participate in a peaceful protest. Completely in solidarity with Catholic social teaching, this organized event attracted derision from passersby. My heart knew that Jesus crucified stood with us that day, and because of this, they didn't irritate my spirit, which stayed firmly at peace. This issue is too important to me, too close to my heart, to let insults dissuade me or tempt me into retaliation. We were unpopular but at peace. Perhaps our simple protest would make a difference. In the kingdom of God, there was rejoicing that day.

1 Corinthians 7:25–31
Psalm 45:11–12,14–15,16–17
Luke 6:20–26

Thursday

SEPTEMBER 8

• THE NATIVITY OF THE BLESSED VIRGIN MARY •

The LORD says:
You, Bethlehem-Ephrathah,
too small to be among the clans of Judah,
From you shall come forth for me
one who is to be ruler in Israel.
—MICAH 5:1

You have no idea what it's like for us who live in first-century
Bethlehem. Our town is close to the Dead Sea, which is the
lowest elevation on the entire earth. We get snow in winter,
and summers are arid and clear. We are overshadowed by
Jerusalem, the great city to the north whose name means
house of peace. If only peace reigned right now. Did you
know our town's name means house of bread? It came true
with Jesus, who was crucified yet rose from the dead. We
proclaim Jesus now. Our Lord is peace itself! Micah said *he*
shall be peace. But Jesus is also bread of life, hope, and love.

Micah 5:1–4a or Romans 8:28–30
Psalm 13:6ab,6c
Matthew 1:1–16,18–23 or 1:18–23

Friday

SEPTEMBER 9

• ST. PETER CLAVER, PRIEST •

I do not fight as if I were shadowboxing.
No, I drive my body and train it.
—1 CORINTHIANS 9:26–27

Our bodies must be trained not to fall into traps of lust, gluttony, and other bodily temptations. These are serious battles. Two saints celebrated today clashed with invisible enemies.

St. Peter Claver fought horrific treatment of enslaved persons and ministered against all odds. Blessed Frederic Ozanam, founder of the St. Vincent de Paul Society, fought poverty in France after being challenged to demonstrate his faith through works. He died on the birthday of Mary, whose heart Simeon prophesied would be pierced by swords. Following Christ is certainly not shadowboxing.

1 Corinthians 9:16–19,22b–27
Psalm 84:3,4,5–6,12
Luke 6:39–42

SEPTEMBER 10

How shall I make a return to the LORD
for all the good he has done for me?
—PSALM 116:12

"How can I ever repay you?" John needed a ride to an important job interview when his car suddenly died. His neighbor saw him out front, panicking over the vehicle. "I can easily get you there. I'll bring my work along and wait for you." Kindnesses that people do don't need to be repaid. But pride hampers the ability to accept free gifts without wanting to offer payback. Kindness has no shelf life; it never spoils. God doesn't need to be repaid but certainly loves expressions of gratitude. It's never too late to say thanks. Nor is it ever too late to pay it forward in service to others.

1 Corinthians 10:14–22
Psalm 116:12–13,17–18
Luke 6:43–49

SEPTEMBER 11

• TWENTY-FOURTH SUNDAY IN ORDINARY TIME •

He became angry,
and when he refused to enter the house,
his father came out and pleaded with him.
—LUKE 15:28

Margaret looked around at Mass and thought, "Boy, are we the older brothers." All these years everyone in this assembly had been faithful, coming weekly to Mass and keeping the commandments. Was Jesus really going to forgive outrageous evildoers on their deathbeds? "I hate to think that; I want more reward or acknowledgment for being faithful." Her eye fell on the Scripture and a line leapt out: "You are here with me always; everything I have is yours." Margaret heard the words as if God spoke them directly to her. Love overpowered her. *Everything God has? Always I will be with God and God with me?* The feeling of being loved took the foreground. A party and a fatted calf for someone else in no way diminished how precious she was to God. God came out to meet her.

Exodus 32:7–11,13–14
Psalm 51:3–4,12–13,17,19
1 Timothy 1:12–17
Luke 15:1–32 or 15:1–10

SEPTEMBER 12

• THE MOST HOLY NAME OF MARY •

When he heard about Jesus, [the centurion] sent elders
of the Jews to him,
asking him to come and save the life of his slave.
—LUKE 7:3

Did you notice that the centurion and Jesus never meet?
First, the Roman sends Jewish leaders to advocate for him.
Based on their testimony, Jesus agrees to go to the centurion.
Jewish elders usually get a bad rap in Scripture, but here they
clearly believe Jesus can heal. They intercede for the
outsider. Do they understand the deeper message of
Christianity that Paul underscores: salvation is for all people?
The centurion doesn't leave his home; he sends friends while
Jesus is en route to say, "I don't consider myself worthy to
come to you, nor are we worthy to have you enter our
home." That is humility. Jesus is amazed. The elders' and
friends' intercessory actions matter.

1 Corinthians 11:17–26,33
Psalm 40:7–8a,8b–9,10,17
Luke 7:1–10

SEPTEMBER 13

• ST. JOHN CHRYSOSTOM, BISHOP AND DOCTOR OF THE CHURCH •

Jesus journeyed to a city called Nain,
and his disciples and a large crowd accompanied him.
As he drew near to the gate of the city,
a man who had died was being carried out,
the only son of his mother, and she was a widow.
A large crowd from the city was with her.
—LUKE 7:11–12

Picture yourself in one of these crowds. Jesus is followed by disciples (not just twelve; probably another seventy-two referred to in chapter 10, and maybe more). As Jesus approaches the city, another large crowd is leaving it. Are you in this merging group? See the widow, the procession, and lots of people. Are you one of those grieving? A compassionate friend? A bystander? Where does Jesus call you to be during this day? You participate in resurrection hope. Whom will you accompany?

1 Corinthians 12:12–14,27–31a
Psalm 100:1b–2,3,4,5
Luke 7:11–17

SEPTEMBER 14

• THE EXALTATION OF THE HOLY CROSS •

Though he was in the form of God,
[Jesus] did not regard equality with God
something to be grasped.
Rather, he emptied himself.
—PHILIPPIANS 2:6–7

The word *exaltation* implies joy. How does that reconcile with divinity hiding itself to suffer in a completely human way? Jesus felt complex human emotions, excruciating pain during physical torture, and mental temptations to give in or give up. Jesus was truly a man and, like other humans, possessed the ability to focus on the goal as a way to push through impossible physical demands. Jesus endured through pure love, knowing his actions meant future celebrations in heaven. Jesus knew that God didn't send him to earth to condemn anyone but rather that everyone would have the opportunity to be saved through Jesus' complete self-giving. That's triumphant and worthy of jubilation.

Numbers 21:4b–9
Psalm 78:1bc–2,34–35,36–37,38
Philippians 2:6–11
John 3:13–17

*Standing by the cross of Jesus were his mother
and his mother's sister, Mary the wife of Clopas,
and Mary Magdalene.*
—JOHN 19:25

Mary leans upon other women, who remain with her to
witness a terrifying execution. What powerful character it
must have taken to watch the slow death of someone they
loved so much. Names are given for fewer than fifty women
in the Bible, contrasted with close to two thousand men.
Suffice it to say, these women were important. Imagine
Mary's elbows being held on either side by a sisterly friend,
lending all her support to Mary so that Mary could maintain
her gaze on her Son, giving him their combined strength.
Christ the man looked upon his mother. He must have been
encouraged knowing she would not be alone.

1 Corinthians 15:1–11
Psalm 118:1b–2,16ab–17,28
John 19:25–27 or Luke 2:33–35

I call upon you, for you will answer me, O God;
incline your ear to me; hear my word.
—PSALM 17:6

While the psalmist seems to make a bold statement of faith that the Lord will definitely respond to prayers, in the very next line the writer requests that the Almighty turn an ear, as if to say, "Hello? Are you really listening?" Faith in God responding seems to be on a continuum, where previous experience lends strength to the belief. Perhaps a prior rescue gives credence to the request. The psalmist seems to be running from some enemy. It could be an inner temptation or a bad habit. Reminding oneself of God's past assistance strengthens faith that God will answer again. Lean on experience. Faith is augmented by prior knowledge.

1 Corinthians 15:12–20
Psalm 17:1bcd,6–7,8b and 15
Luke 8:1–3

[Jesus said,] "The seed is the word of God."
—LUKE 8:11B

In profligate abandon, God spreads the seeds of love far and
wide. Time and again, the seed seeks places to thrive, but it
finds inhospitable paths, rocky terrain, and patches full of
weeds. Seeds are expensive. They're precious, like God's Son,
who is the Word. God doesn't quit despite the hostile
response. The divine farmer keeps sowing and even enlists
companions to join in planting with excessive generosity. Are
you one of the sower's friends, or do you see yourself as an
employee, and if so, what does your technique of seed
distribution look like? The word keeps going out. A word
you sow today may multiply into God's wisdom to be
harvested by others.

1 Corinthians 15:35–37,42–49
Psalm 56:10c–12,13–14
Luke 8:4–15

Sunday

SEPTEMBER 18

• TWENTY-FIFTH SUNDAY IN ORDINARY TIME •

*I ask that supplications, prayers,
petitions, and thanksgivings be made for everyone,
for kings and for all in authority.*
—1 TIMOTHY 2:1–2

Paul nailed it when he recommended prayers for everyone in leadership, whether we agree with them or not. If we pull out our tape measures and fret when decision makers don't measure up, it's better to pray with every possible tool in our prayer belt. Wrench complaining out of your psyche by turning it into praise. Wedge in small penances, such as skipping snacks between meals or favorite beverages for a week. Hammer away at God with persistent petitions. Turning the screws on differences will only get you upset. Bracket your prayers with gratitude. Invest in the proper tools, and you just might build yourself a place a peace. And a world of difference.

Amos 8:4–7
Psalm 113:1–2,4–6,7–8
1 Timothy 2:1–8
Luke 16:1–13 or 16:10–13

SEPTEMBER 19

• ST. JANUARIUS, BISHOP AND MARTYR •

There is nothing hidden that will not become visible,
and nothing secret that will not be known
and come to light.
—LUKE 8:17

Secret keeping is attractive, especially when it's about a mistake made or an embarrassing situation endured. People say things to themselves in the secret of their hearts that they would never say to someone else. "You're worthless" or "You're a failure" are the kinds of secret statements best called out for what they are: evil tricks to diminish a precious image of God. Evil plots to hide goodness will not succeed in the long run. Clandestine thoughts of negativity can snowball if left unchecked. Better to increase self-awareness of invisible statements that slip into your mind. God wills only your good, and God's goodness cannot be hidden.

Proverbs 3:27–34
Psalm 15:2–3a,3bc–4ab,5
Luke 8:16–18

SEPTEMBER 20

• ST. ANDREW KIM TAEGON, PRIEST, AND ST. PAUL CHONG HASANG, AND
COMPANIONS, MARTYRS •

He who shuts his ear to the cry of the poor
will himself also call and not be heard.
—PROVERBS 21:13

It seems like the parable of the rich man who died and entered
torment would be a good pairing with this verse. Lazarus, who
epitomized poverty, was welcomed to the bosom of Abraham
while the rich man could only cry out from his place across the
abyss. He wanted to be heard—and he wanted his family to
hear and thus get another chance. No such luck. In modern
culture, people crave to be heard, to be in positions of power,
while they themselves do not listen. In today's Gospel, Jesus
says that the ones who hear the cry of the poor are the ones
who are most closely related to him.

Proverbs 21:1–6,10–13
Psalm 119:1,27,30,34,35,44
Luke 8:19–21

Wednesday

SEPTEMBER 21

• ST. MATTHEW, APOSTLE AND EVANGELIST •

*[Jesus said,] "Those who are well do not need a physician,
but the sick do."*
—MATTHEW 9:12B

Jesus still makes house calls. He seeks people who are ill,
especially those sickened by failures to love. But there are
those who say, "I don't need a doctor; I'm fine," after
describing excruciating pain. They reject calls from the
divine Doctor who wants to set up an appointment.
Sometimes the rejection is out of misplaced fear: what if the
diagnosis is fourth stage and incurable? "Fear not!" says Jesus
at every turn. God will heal, provide a way out, or offer the
strength to endure. Admitting the need for Jesus the Doctor
requires a willingness to admit we are powerless to fix
ourselves and the world around us. In Ephesians, St. Paul
offers a prescription: exercise humility, gentleness, patience,
and striving for unity. The best medicine is love.

Ephesians 4:1–7,11–13
Psalm 19:2–3,4–5
Matthew 9:9–13

SEPTEMBER 22

[Herod asked,] "Who then is this about whom I hear such things?"
And he kept trying to see [Jesus].
—LUKE 9:9B

In 2022, information circumnavigates the globe in seconds. It wouldn't take long, for example, for Mexico City to be overrun if news reported that miracles were suddenly flooding from the Basilica of Our Lady of Guadalupe. Like Herod, people crave to know about the latest surprising phenomena. What's truly important may be more difficult to decipher. Much of what attracts attention on social media is "vanity of vanities." News of superficialities soon fades. Jesus' miracles carried long-lasting impact. Hearts changed. Lives were converted. We are invited to do likewise. There are actions we can undertake today that will draw curious minds to seek out information about Jesus.

Ecclesiastes 1:2–11
Psalm 90:3–4,5–6,12–13,14 and 17bc
Luke 9:7–9

"Then [Jesus] said to them, "But who do you say that I am?"
—LUKE 9:20

Have you ever overheard a friend telling someone about you?
Your ears perked up. Like any person, Jesus could have been
curious. He may have known other people's thoughts but
wanted to hear his friends put it into their own words. Jesus
was leader, respected teacher, awe-inspiring commander,
mysterious miracle worker, and more. He was Mary's Son,
among other things. Don't you imagine Mary talking to
people about who her Son was? She may have had
expectations of how Jesus would fulfill his mission. Perhaps
Jesus surprised her. Was he a spitting image of his mother's
side of the family? Today you will have an opportunity to be
Jesus for someone. It may even be for yourself. As an image
of God, your life shares the familial resemblance.

Ecclesiastes 3:1–11
Psalm 144:1b and 2abc, 3–4
Luke 9:18–22

SEPTEMBER 24

Prosper the work of our hands!
—PSALM 90:17

God never stops laboring alongside human beings, but God's
coworkers may have quite different goals than God does.
People like success and getting results, and it's no fun when
projects are scrapped and all efforts appear pointless.
However, God looks at the process as much as the end result.
Even when efforts seem fruitless, God wastes nothing. A
children's craft project that consumes their energy for hours,
develops fine motor skills, and builds patience may be
thrown away, but the intangibles remain. Our souls are
always learning, growing, and pulling closer to love. Never
give up, even when it seems that your work doesn't prosper.

Ecclesiastes 11:9—12:8
Psalm 90:3–4,5–6,12–13,14 and 17
Luke 9:43b–45

SEPTEMBER 25

Thus says the LORD the God of hosts:
Woe to the complacent in Zion!
—AMOS 6:1A

On a recent national holiday Monica would rather have stayed home in bed or checked social media. She heard a nagging voice in the back of her head: *What difference will one more person make in a march for justice? Why bother? There will be plenty of other people to stand up. You deserve rest.* She almost gave in to the lukewarm attitude. But she recognized discouragement in the making and decided to act against it. She dragged herself to the nearby parish parking lot to participate in the march. She saw enthusiastic sign-wavers and happy children. The sunshine felt good, and so did the exercise. She stood together with others who filled the streets to speak up for justice. Peace filled her. She was glad she went.

Amos 6:1a,4–7
Psalm 146:7,8–9,9–10 (1b)
1 Timothy 6:11–16
Luke 16:19–31

*[Jesus said,] "Whoever receives this child in my name receives me,
and whoever receives me receives the one
who sent me."*
—LUKE 9:48

Today's martyrs were surely friends, and possibly brothers. In
the United States today, some folks celebrate National Good
Neighbor Day. The story of the Good Samaritan will be part of
the readings next Monday. No need to wait, however, to be a
blessing to someone you know, or to someone you don't. Try
something out of the ordinary: greet a neighbor you never talk
to. Smile and say hello to a stranger on the sidewalk. Take time
for a coworker you barely know. See if you can do a neighborly
deed. People in proximity may surprise you when you get to
know them. Every time you connect with another person, you
receive a chance to see the face of God.

Job 1:6–22
Psalm 17:1bcd,2–3,6–7
Luke 9:46–50

Tuesday

SEPTEMBER 27

• ST. VINCENT DE PAUL, PRIEST •

*[Jesus said,] "The harvest is abundant but the laborers are few;
so ask the master of the harvest
to send out laborers for his harvest."*
—MATTHEW 9:37–38

Jesus wants us to ask. To do that, we must identify what it is
we want to ask *for*. It may be the grace to face a stressful job,
patience with a sick relative, or help with a particularly tough
situation. God loves when we ask for graces to make the
laboring in life more fruitful. Jesus calls his Abba the head of
the harvest. This connotes fall festivals and pumpkins.
Rejoicing! Let's think about our lives as fields, ready and
abundant. What does a rich heart-harvest look like?

MEMORIAL
1 Corinthians 1:26–31
Psalm 112:1bc–2,3–4,5–6,7–8,9
Matthew 9:35–38

SEPTEMBER 28

• ST. WENCESLAUS, MARTYR • ST. LAWRENCE RUIZ AND COMPANIONS,
MARTYRS •

God is wise in heart and mighty in strength;
who has withstood him and remained unscathed?
—JOB 9:4

What image comes immediately to mind when you consider
God? Job imaged God as Creator, who made the
constellations. The psalmist today images God as a
wonder-worker who seems to have forgotten those who call
out in prayer. Jesus is the image of the invisible God, and he
issues a radical call to follow, at the expense of familial
relationships if necessary. What kind of God allows the
sickening torture that ended the lives of St. Lawrence Ruiz
and other martyrs in Japan? God is the giver of free choice, a
dangerous and powerful gift. Our wise and mighty God is
incomprehensible mystery.

Job 9:1–12,14–16
Psalm 88:10bc–11,12–13,14–15
Luke 9:57–62

SEPTEMBER 29

• ST. MICHAEL, ST. GABRIEL, AND ST. RAPHAEL, ARCHANGELS •

*[Jesus said,] "You will see heaven opened
and the angels of God ascending and descending."*
—JOHN 1:51

Do you believe in angels? Jesus did. Children's companion
angels, Jesus said, always behold God's face (Matthew 18:10).
Angels ministered to Jesus after his temptations (Matthew
4:11). Modern society relegates angels to fantasies or depicts
them as harmless cherubs. It's likely that angels are mighty
warriors fearful in appearance. Why else would good people
like Mary feel terrified at their sudden presence? Angels
appear frequently in the Hebrew Scriptures. Re-imagining
angels and their roles as God's messengers can yield great
food for prayer. Because every person is a child of God, it
makes sense that every person has a guarding angel. If saints
can intercede, why not guardian angels?

Daniel 7:9–10,13–14 or Revelation 12:7–12a
Psalm 138:1–2ab,2cde–3,4–5
John 1:47–51

I give you thanks that I am fearfully, wonderfully made;
wonderful are your works.
—PSALM 139:14

Nobody knows me like you do, God. You know me better than I know myself. I may think that I can hide from you, but you see everything. How you must smile when I try to conceal anything from you. I'm good at refusing to see things about myself. I may not be aware that you are there, but you are always present and in all things and circumstances. Oh, how I take you for granted, as I do every breath and every heartbeat! I forget that you hold all. Wake me up to your holy presence. Stir in me the realization that you made me good, valuable, and—thanks to Jesus—worthy of you, imperfect sinner that I am.

Job 38:1,12–21; 40:3–5
Psalm 139:1–3,7–8,9–10,13–14ab
Luke 10:13–16

Saturday

OCTOBER 1

• ST. THÉRÈSE OF THE CHILD JESUS, VIRGIN AND DOCTOR OF THE CHURCH •

I busy not myself with great things,
nor with things too sublime for me.
Nay, rather, I have stilled and quieted
my soul like a weaned child.
—PSALM 131:1DE-2

God is like the mother of a seven-year-old who's spending a week away from home at summer camp for the first time. Mom isn't there, but the child leans on faith, knowing Mom will greet her at week's end. Girls at Teresita Pines sang loudly as they walked through the dark forest to their cabins after the nightly campfire, "St. Theresa, St. Theresa, I have placed my trust in thee. Though you have so many children, pray especially for me. When the clouds begin to gather and the sun has gone to hide, won't you help me in my troubles? St. Theresa be my guide." St. Therese's little way leads homesick souls to God our Mother when dark times threaten.

MEMORIAL
Isaiah 66:10–14c
Psalm 131:1bcde,2,3
Matthew 18:1–4

OCTOBER 2

Write down the vision clearly upon the tablets.
—HABAKKUK 2:2

To live an intentional life involves having a vision of where we're heading. Without goals, hopes, and dreams, how will we know if we've arrived at where we want to be? And how do we know what to value and what deserves an investment of time? When we take our plans to Jesus and prayerfully open ourselves to God's feedback, some course corrections may be necessary. In the long run, the plan will be better for us and for others. Together with God, we work on plans that fit our talents, family situations, times, and places. Habakkuk encourages us even now to stick by our visions, to work for and wait for them, and to believe that God is in charge. The vision will surely come.

Habakkuk 1:2–3; 2:2–4
Psalm 95:1–2,6–7,8–9 (8)
2 Timothy 1:6–8,13–14
Luke 17:5–10

[The scholar asked,] "And who is my neighbor?"
—LUKE 10:29B

Few people know who lives in the apartment or house next
door or down the street. Perhaps we occasionally smile or
wave, but our neighbors remain largely strangers. People pull
into garages and quickly shut the automatic doors. To shout a
hello feels awkward. Perhaps there's fear that if we know the
neighbors, they may need something from us. It might
involve forming a relationship, and those take work, time,
and energy. Or there are grudges or irritations festering from
some not-so-neighborly incident years ago. It's time to get
over it. Someone in our neighborhood needs us to reach out.
It may take a special request for God's grace to bravely knock
on a door, offer cookies or home-grown produce, and dare to
be thought crazy for going against a culture's individualistic
mentality that keeps people apart.

Galatians 1:6–12
Psalm 111:1b–2,7–8,9 and 10c
Luke 10:25–37

Tuesday
OCTOBER 4

• ST. FRANCIS OF ASSISI •

I bear the marks of Jesus on my body.
—GALATIANS 6:17

It is said that St. Francis of Assisi bore the stigmata—the same
physical wounds that Jesus has from the cross. Before you
judge how extraordinary that was, remember that you also
bear Christ's wounds in your body. It comes with being human.
Both you and Christ suffer shortcomings like physical sickness
and broken bones. In addition, there are wounds of betrayal by
friends, mocking put-downs, and undeserved ridicule. Jesus
bore the pains of loneliness, uncertainty, and suffering. Jesus
saw Mary sorrowing at the foot of his cross. You, too, are
privileged to bear the marks of Christ in whatever heartache
you endure. Not all wounds are visible.

MEMORIAL
Galatians 6:14–18
Psalm 16:1b–2a and 5,7–8,11
Matthew 11:25–30

Wednesday

OCTOBER 5

Father, hallowed be your name,
your kingdom come.
Give us each day our daily bread
and forgive us our sins
for we ourselves forgive everyone in debt to us,
and do not subject us to the final test.
—LUKE 11:2B–4

St. Ignatius suggests praying a single word of the Our Father per one inhalation and exhalation. Slow it down. Make room for God to speak between the words. It's a method for savoring a prayer Jesus used when his disciples asked him to teach them how to pray. Sink into a single thought, let your racing mind empty, and repeat that one word for additional breaths if needed. Stay with it as long as it deserves attention. Stop for several minutes on an idea or word as God moves you to do so. Watch for and hear something new by slowing down this familiar prayer.

Galatians 2:1–2,7–14
Psalm 117:1bc,2
Luke 11:1–4

Thursday

OCTOBER 6

• ST. BRUNO, PRIEST • BLESSED MARIE-ROSE DUROCHER, VIRGIN •

Blessed be the Lord, the God of Israel;
he has come to his people.
—LUKE 1:68

Counting every blessing is impossible—every life has too
many to count. Why is it difficult to remember this and so
effortless to feel complacent or entitled? When thoughts
focus on problems, complaints bubble up rather than thanks.
Some people keep gratitude journals, a discipline that fosters
an appreciative heart. It's possible to be grateful for little
blessings, like apple juice, gas in the car, toothpaste, and a
photo. Some blessings, like a spouse, are so big they could be
listed every day. The greatest blessing ever? Jesus. God is
revealing divine presence in every day, but a heart that isn't
grateful just may miss it. Time to ask, what gets in the way of
gratitude today?

Galatians 3:1–5
Luke 1:69–70,71–72,73–75
Luke 11:5–13

"Hail, full of grace! The Lord is with you."
—LUKE 1:28

A rosary isn't only for Hail Marys. You can repeat any words you want. With my granddaughter, new to the practice, we repeated, "I love you, Jesus" ten times, and for the Our Father, we used, "Thank you, God, for loving me." It was a way to ease her into a new habit of meditation. I felt humbled as I listened to her pray. We hung her rosary on the bedpost where it would be easy to find at night, especially if she woke from a scary dream. My mother used to say that if I fell asleep during the rosary, my guardian angel would finish it for me. Any psalm could also substitute for Hail Marys. Today I will repeat, "God, your works are to be treasured."

MEMORIAL
Acts 1:12–14
Luke 1:46–47, 48–49, 50–51, 52–53, 54–55
Luke 1:26–38

OCTOBER 8

Look to the LORD in his strength;
seek to serve him constantly.
—PSALM 105:4

If I seek to serve God at all times, I can expect God to provide the necessary strength to endure whatever comes. God's agenda is my gauge for choosing how to spend my time. What of all the myriad things I could do today does God want me to tackle, and tackle first? Unfortunately, I often pray backwards: God, let's start with my agenda, things I want to do; please give me strength to accomplish them so people will appreciate me and my successes. Serving God means doing the opposite. Pray first, and then act out of the inspirations that arise from it.

Galatians 3:22–29
Psalm 105:2–3,4–5,6–7
Luke 11:27–28

Sunday

OCTOBER 9

• TWENTY-EIGHTH SUNDAY IN ORDINARY TIME •

[Jesus said,] "Your faith has saved you."
—LUKE 17:19

What happened later to the other nine lepers? God could have taken back their healings, but I doubt he did. God most likely allowed them to live full, healthy lives, in which they retold the story of their miraculous cures regularly. As the second reading says, if we're unfaithful, Jesus remains faithful, for he cannot deny himself. No doubt the human side of Jesus wanted appreciation. It's a normal human desire. Come to think of it, it's what God wants most from people: gratitude. Being recipients of thanks is one of the ways we are made in the image of God. Our response of appreciation is a natural outcome of Jesus walking among us still. God hears prayers through us and responds. It's our place of dignity. We were created to receive and bestow gratitude.

2 Kings 5:14–17
Psalm 98:1,2–3,3–4
2 Timothy 2:8–13
Luke 17:11–19

Monday
OCTOBER 10

For freedom Christ set us free;
so stand firm and do not submit again
to the yoke of slavery.
—GALATIANS 5:1

During a tug-of-war, the winning side digs in their heels and
stands firm. What helps you dig in your heels when tempted
to fall back into habitual dysfunctions? A quick, one-word
prayer—"Help!"—can be repeated again and again when
we're tempted to choose poorly. Prayer may feel like the last
thing on your mind in the heat of a tempting moment. Dig in
your heels. Grip that rope of Christ with a simple word.
Don't let team slavery tug you over to the losing side. Be
patient as you pray. Help from Christ will surely come.
Exercise your prayer biceps and quads; they will get stronger.
You'll be surprised by the endurance you build within.

Galatians 4:22–24,26–27,31—5:1
Psalm 113:1b–2,3–4,5a and 6–7
Luke 11:29–32

Tuesday

OCTOBER 11

• ST. JOHN XXIII, POPE •

Let your mercy come to me, O LORD.
—PSALM 119:41A

Notice who is doing the heavy lifting in the psalm: God. All
we must do is let God in. Allow the God whose name is
Mercy do what God does best: love us and forgive us. Watch
to see God's compassion manifest. Don't be afraid! Don't
withhold yourself from God. Fear sometimes gets the upper
hand. It doesn't have to. Stand up to it, and let God's merciful
love come! We don't deserve or earn God's generosity and
clemency. All is gift.

Galatians 5:1–6
Psalm 119:41,43,44,45,47,48
Luke 11:37–41

OCTOBER 12

*The fruit of the Spirit is love, joy, peace,
patience, kindness, generosity,
faithfulness, gentleness, self-control.*
—GALATIANS 5:22

Look at all that fruit! What a bumper crop. Near Sacramento at
this time of year, people flock to Apple Hill for fresh produce
and lush fall color as leaves change. Picture the Holy Spirit
offering free bushel baskets of joy. She's got eight additional
varieties of fruits among her harvest, colorfully bright in
contrast to the rotting fruit of discord in the next bin. Paul
shopped at this market frequently, and he planted seeds for
others to harvest also. Look around! Reap autumn's gifts.
Winter will come, and you will need to store up strength in
your cellar. Which fruit is your favorite? For which would you
be willing to pay a high price to the Grower?

Galatians 5:18–25
Psalm 1:1–2,3,4 and 6
Luke 11:42–46

Thursday

OCTOBER 13

[Jesus said,] "Woe to you, scholars of the law!
You have taken away the key of knowledge."
—LUKE 11:52

Imagine the reactions of Pharisees who just got blasted after
providing a delicious, perhaps expensive, meal on their best
dishes. Perhaps Jesus speaks harshly as a way of trying to
shake them out of complacency. Prophets of the past spoke
vehemently, too. It was a matter of God-life and death.
"Pharisees" exist in our day also, spouting law over love.
Being in a leadership position, whether as a trusted mentor or
family member, means watching out for legalisms, hasty
judgments, and ostracizing behaviors. Jesus offers the key of
knowledge, the Holy Spirit, and it may require a serious
course correction to accept it.

Ephesians 1:1–10
Psalm 98:1,2–3ab,3cd–4,5–6
Luke 11:47–54

Friday

OCTOBER 14

• ST. CALLISTUS I, POPE AND MARTYR •

Tend the flock of God in your midst,
overseeing it not by constraint but willingly,
as God would have it.
—1 PETER 5:2

Just off the old Appian Way in Rome and up a rough driveway lined with tall trees are the catacombs of St. Callistus. Close your eyes and spend some time feeling the dry warmth of an autumn day as the simple path silently points the way. Give yourself a pilgrimage moment. Try to journey from head to heart. Think about what you see and hear in this tranquil spot. Christian ancestors prayed here. Underground they sang and celebrated Mass among the remains of martyrs. St. Callistus was caretaker of this cemetery, famous among Rome's ancient burial places. To this day, the catacombs are well-cared-for holy ground. Over what can you exert great care today and leave as a legacy?

MEMORIAL
1 Peter 5:1–4
Psalm 40:2 and 4ab,7–8a,8b–9,10,11
Luke 22:24–30

For who hopes for what one sees?
But if we hope for what we do not see,
we wait with endurance.
—ROMANS 8:24B–25

St. Teresa, like many people today, lived a remarkably busy life. She still made time to pen *The Way of Perfection*. Writing specifically for nuns, St. Teresa didn't worry about trying to make her sentences perfect. She wrote as a mother to her daughters, encouraging them never to fear that God would fail them. She saw herself, and them, as precious castles where God resides; heaven can be found within. She couldn't foresee her writings becoming classics. She wrote with purpose. Journaling can be a purposeful form of prayer. Record an imaginary dialogue with God. Or send a letter to someone who is like a daughter to you, or like a spiritual parent.

MEMORIAL
Romans 8:22–27
Psalm 19:8,9,10,11
John 15:1–8

Sunday

OCTOBER 16

• TWENTY-NINTH SUNDAY IN ORDINARY TIME •

Moses' hands, however, grew tired. . . .
Aaron and Hur supported his hands,
one on one side and one on the other.
—EXODUS 17:12

Hold out your arms as if you were on a cross. Time how long you hold this position before your arms become tired. Who supports you when your prayer needs a lift? Reflect on someone who "rolled a rock in place" for you to sit on and then helped hold up your arms as you followed the path that you knew God was asking you to walk. Sometimes God's call is difficult, and you need the prayerful support of an Aaron and a Hur to keep you faithful, to give you strength, and to encourage you when you're too tired or tempted to go it alone. After spending time in quiet reflection, give God thanks for these supports.

Exodus 17:8–13
Psalm 121:1–2,3–4,5–6,7–8
2 Timothy 3:14—4:2
Luke 18:1–8

Monday

OCTOBER 17

• ST. IGNATIUS OF ANTIOCH, BISHOP AND MARTYR •

Stand firm in the Lord, beloved.
—PHILIPPIANS 4:1

This St. Ignatius was a Syrian convert to the faith who valued unity and fidelity to Christ at all costs. How close his name is to the word *ignite*! He died in the Roman Colosseum. No possessions were as important to him as his fortitude in following Christ. In a few days, the readings will quote Jesus, "I have come to set the earth on fire, and how I wish it were already blazing! There is a baptism with which I must be baptized, and how great is my anguish until it is accomplished!" (Luke 12:49). Today's saint shared Christ's determination and zeal.

MEMORIAL
Philippians 3:17—4:1
Psalm 34:2–3, 4–5, 6–7, 8–9
John 12:24–26

OCTOBER 18

• ST. LUKE, EVANGELIST •

Whatever town you enter, and they welcome you,
eat what is set before you.
—LUKE 10:9

Jesus sent scouts, or perhaps heralds, to places he would soon visit. He missioned seventy-two people with instructions to travel light and to value simplicity. Consider what city dwellers thought as disciples arrived to alert them that the reign of God was imminent. Curing sick people would certainly be a big proof of the validity of their message. Hope would blossom that the Messiah was on the way. Soon Jesus himself would visit, with a story about a persistent widow (Luke 18:1–8) as an example of how to pray. Jesus would compare God to a woman who lost a coin (Luke 15:8–10) as an example of how a lavish God turns her house upside down looking for that one sinner. (These two stories appear only in Luke's Gospel.)

2 Timothy 4:10–17b
Psalm 145:10–11,12–13,17–18
Luke 10:1–9

> *The mystery of Christ . . .*
> *[is] that the Gentiles are coheirs, members of the*
> *same Body.*
> —EPHESIANS 3:4B, 6A

This is fantastic news. It's definitely worth smiling over, because whatever your origins, you belong. You are part of God's eternal family. Imagine the face of Jesus looking at you right now. Picture him with the start of a grin creeping across his face. Jesus is looking at you, and he is breaking out in a smile. His eyes gleam. Jesus likes what he sees. You are a beloved friend. Jesus is happy to see you every day, no matter the circumstances. Spend some time letting Jesus look at you, smiling.

Ephesians 3:2–12
Isaiah 12:2–3,4bcd,5–6
Luke 12:39–48

Thursday

OCTOBER 20

• ST. PAUL OF THE CROSS, PRIEST •

[Jesus said,] "I have come to set the earth on fire,
and how I wish it were already blazing!
There is a baptism with which I must be baptized,
and how great is my anguish until it is accomplished!"
—LUKE 12:49–50

If you've been writing notes on previous pages as suggested in
the Introduction, consider rereading some that you starred.
You can deepen graces received by engaging in a repetition of
prayers where God and you encountered each other. Try
reviewing the Scriptures for October 17 to see if St. Ignatius of
Antioch helped you recommit to zeal for following Christ. Ask
yourself, in what situation(s) have I demonstrated courage in
speaking up about Jesus, despite expected negative
consequences? Have I risked a blazing fire of suffering as a
path to a new baptism, a new submersion in love?

Ephesians 3:14–21
Psalm 33:1–2,4–5,11–12,18–19
Luke 12:49–53

Friday

OCTOBER 21

Such is the race that seeks for him
That seeks for the face of the God of Jacob.
—PSALM 24:6

In the Old Testament context, "seeing God's face" translates into a person's life on earth being over—no one could see God's face and live. Am I ready to die today? Are you? As this liturgical year ages, the readings speak more and more about the end times. As I wait for the end of earthly life, how am I supposed to wait well? The second reading recommends exercising patience, which is a great tool against desolation when darkness sneaks up. At this moment, I'd rather be invited to patience while I continue living fully, and be invited to experience joy and gratitude for what I have. For now, I want to meet Christ in the countenances of people here and now. I ask for the graces to be ready to die if the day comes sooner than I hope it will.

Ephesians 4:1–6
Psalm 24:1–2,3–4ab,5–6
Luke 12:54–59

OCTOBER 22

• ST. JOHN PAUL II, POPE •

[Jesus said,] "Do you think that because these Galileans suffered
in this way
they were greater sinners than all other Galileans?
By no means!
—LUKE 13:2B–3A

People who lived through World War II knew of atrocities on a
massive scale. As a clandestine seminary student, the pope
honored today hid in a basement while guards searched for
clergy to ship them to concentration camps or immediately
execute them. Karol Wojtyla persevered through perils of
many kinds, including a near-fatal traffic accident. Suffering
happens to everybody in varying degrees, but it's not divine
punishment. God allows people to choose badly, and God lets
the consequences of such behaviors hurt the innocent. Misery
is still a mystery. May God provide consolation and courage to
people who will be forced to endure perils that come their way
through no fault of their own.

Ephesians 4:7–16
Psalm 122:1–2,3–4ab,4cd–5
Luke 13:1–9

Sunday

OCTOBER 23

• THIRTIETH SUNDAY IN ORDINARY TIME •

The Lord is a God of justice,
who knows no favorites.
Though not unduly partial toward the weak,
yet he hears the cry of the oppressed.
—SIRACH 35:12–13

A grown child asked his mother which of her children was the favorite. "The one who needs me the most," she replied without hesitation. One adult child was struggling at that moment with all kinds of overwhelming trials. The mother spent extra time and energy supporting this son, who wasn't always interested in receiving such help. God's limitless heart is such that every individual can count on always being the favorite. When a child in God's family needs an additional measure of support, faith teaches that God's help is sufficient and love will prevail.

Sirach 35:12–14,16–18
Psalm 34:2–3,17–18,19,23 (7a)
2 Timothy 4:6–8,16–18
Luke 18:9–14

Monday

OCTOBER 24

• ST. ANTHONY MARY CLARET, BISHOP •

When [Jesus] said this, all his adversaries were humiliated;
and the whole crowd rejoiced at all the splendid
deeds done by him.
—LUKE 13:17

How humiliating to be called a hypocrite in front of others!
In my defense, I was trying to protect the Sabbath from
abuse when I told the crowds to come for healing six other
days a week. But Jesus was right. Of course I untie my
animals for watering. I didn't conflate their needs with this
woman's. I admit to thinking her life was worth little; she
couldn't work or contribute to society. My animals had more
value. But Jesus saw her dignity, crippled as she was. In
retrospect, I see that I judged her by what she could do, not
by who she was: an image of God regardless of her ability to
contribute to society.

Ephesians 4:32—5:8
Psalm 1:1–2,3,4 and 6
Luke 13:10–17

Tuesday

OCTOBER 25

Jesus said, "What is the Kingdom of God like?"
—LUKE 13:18

We ought to know. Jesus tells us that the reign of God is already among us. The reign involves an attitude of love, a viewpoint of finding God in everything, and much more. How would you describe it? In the Eucharist, Jesus brings the reign of God into our very bodies. The metaphors of a seed and yeast hint that the reign starts out small. Jesus, after all, began in an insignificant town, amassed merely twelve apostles, and died a criminal's death. But the reign of God was already among us, in Jesus, our Emmanuel, whose name means "God with us." Through the Spirit, the early church grew exponentially. Given time and the right environment, yeast will transform simple ingredients. And so will God's reign among us. Watch for it.

Ephesians 5:21–33
Psalm 128:1–2,3,4–5
Luke 13:18–21

*And there will be wailing and grinding of teeth
when you see Abraham, Isaac, and Jacob
and all the prophets in the Kingdom of God
and you yourselves cast out.*
—LUKE 13:28

People who've had extensive dental work cringe at the notion of grinding teeth. Jesus is issuing a warning and a call. Strive for the prize; otherwise expect narrow gates, locked doors, and being asked to leave. Jesus describes a kingdom where those left out can see the party, but they can't participate. Jesus used plenty of images that interconnect. God's reign, like a mustard seed, must be cultivated. Making bread using yeast takes work. Jesus warns that people must try hard for the kingdom. People aren't entitled to it. It's not enough to eat at the communion table; followers of Jesus must serve others, and even carry a cross.

Ephesians 6:1–9
Psalm 145:10–11,12–13ab,13cd–14
Luke 13:22–30

Thursday

OCTOBER 27

*Draw your strength from the Lord and from his
mighty power.*
—EPHESIANS 6:10

"Passion of Christ, strengthen me," reads a line in the *Anima
Christi*, or Soul of Christ prayer. Knowing that a very human
Jesus suffered tremendously while people ridiculed him gives
us strength somehow. Jesus powered through the entire Via
Dolorosa by thinking of humanity. For the sake of the joy
that lay before him, he endured the cross (Hebrews 12:1–2).
Jesus drew his strength from knowing that his suffering had
critical purpose: our salvation. How can we compare our
suffering to what Christ experienced? If he who was innocent
humbled himself to endure excruciating pain, we can be
energized by staying close to Jesus, who endured and forgave
when those who hurt him didn't deserve it.

Ephesians 6:10–20
Psalm 144:1b,2,9–10
Luke 13:31–35

*You are fellow citizens with the holy ones
and members of the household of God.*
—EPHESIANS 2:19B

Belonging is a basic human need. All followers of Jesus,
thanks to a foundation established by generations of
forebears, carry passports to God's country. Citizens who
went before us laid the groundwork for ministries and the
infrastructure for a church that persists, even though it's
broken. Pause for a moment to imagine arriving at heaven's
door and St. Peter is the one in the booth checking
documents. Do you feel confident in the quality of your
paperwork? Rest assured, your citizenship papers are signed
in Christ's blood. We are welcomed in our home country:
God's loving arms.

Ephesians 2:19–22
Psalm 19:2–3,4–5
Luke 6:12–16

*Christ will be magnified in my body,
whether by life or by death.*
—PHILIPPIANS 1:20

What strategies can cultivate Paul's attitude of indifference?
Think for a moment of the hooks that snag you today. It
might be a long to-do list that drags you down when you
can't accomplish everything. If so, you've been tricked into
thinking your value comes from what you do. Maybe you
have quite an attachment to opinions others hold about you.
If so, you forget that only God's judgment counts. You may
have a disordered desire to be physically fit, well-fed, and
attractive. If so, you may be shortening your prayer time to
accomplish transitory bodily gain. None of us can disengage
fully from our dysfunctions or bad habits without God's help.
Ask God to give you a true vision of yourself and knowledge
of how you can magnify the Lord. Talk to Mary, too.

Philippians 1:18b–26
Psalm 42:2,3,5cdef
Luke 14:1,7–11

Jesus came to Jericho and intended
to pass through the town.
—LUKE 19:1

Looking up and seeing Zacchaeus, Jesus changed his mind. He decided not to keep going. "I must stay at your house," Jesus said. It wasn't a request. Surprise! What would be your reaction if you heard Jesus say, "I must stay in your house"? Would you be joyful, as was Zacchaeus? Or would it be, "I'm not ready! Everything must be clean before Jesus arrives. What if Jesus brings others I don't like?" Maybe you were content to observe Jesus from a distance. Now he wants to *stay*? Do you let yourself be seen? Somewhere during your week, Jesus sought you out through others and asked to remain with you. Climb down from your hidden spot. Jesus wants you.

Wisdom 11:22—12:2
Psalm 145:1–2,8–9,10–11,13,14
2 Thessalonians 1:11—2:2
Luke 19:1–10

OCTOBER 31

Do nothing out of selfishness or out of vainglory;
rather, humbly regard others as
more important than yourselves.
—PHILIPPIANS 2:3

Paul writes a tough saying. If I don't put myself first, who
will? Our culture sees vainglory, or excessive pride, as virtue.
There's even a video game named for it. Pride surely causes
desolation eventually. Vanity masks that God is really in
charge. How hard is it to let someone else go first through a
door or to let another take that parking space, without
getting angry? Maybe that person who cut me off is Jesus,
heading to an emergency. I'm not to judge. I cannot control
graces, but I can request them, including the ability to
humbly step back and ask God to let me see others as Jesus.

Philippians 2:1–4
Psalm 131:1bcde,2,3
Luke 14:12–14

I, John, saw another angel come up from the East,
holding the seal of the living God.
—REVELATION 7:2

I opened the front door yesterday to find an angel there. Her halo glowed with light reflected from the jack-o'-lantern. Her billowy gown fell on the porch like a cloud of mist. The angel looked hopefully at me, waiting for a response. I had a choice, and she would accept whatever I chose to give. How many times have angels rung my doorbell? Scripture is full of angels. There were some who behaved angelically for me this past year, including one in disguise and an intercessor who is now dead. I'd like to look back to discover the nameless, unnoticed saints who popped into this week holding a message from my beloved Lord.

Revelation 7:2–4,9–14
Psalm 24:1b–2,3–4ab,5–6
1 John 3:1–3
Matthew 5:1–12a

[Jesus said,] "Do not let your hearts be troubled.
You have faith in God; have faith also in me.
In my Father's house there are many dwelling places."
—JOHN 14:1–2

Day of the Dead *offrendas*, or altars, celebrate the lives of
deceased loved ones—ordinary people well remembered. In
Sacramento, a nonprofit set up a nighttime display where
families and friends created a wide range of memorials
complete with photos, colorful tablecloths, flowers, music,
religious icons, and even dancing. Volunteers dressed in
flowing Hispanic costumes, and, with faces made up like sugar
skulls, prayerfully passed through a votive-lit "graveyard." It
called forth thoughts of resurrection and a joy-filled hereafter.
Not morbid or sad, the effect was celebratory. In faith we know
that special places await us after death. Loving Savior, remove
every fear, especially of the unknown.

Wisdom 3:1–9
Romans 5:5–11 or 6:3–9
John 14:1–6

*I even consider everything as a loss because of the supreme good of
knowing Christ Jesus my Lord.*
—PHILIPPIANS 3:8

Constant service does not mean pridefully overworking, as if
the world depended upon one human being (other than
Jesus, of course). Overwork is a sickness that society
considers a virtue. Service best begins from a call in which
God provides strength and energy. How do people know if
God is inviting them to prioritize a particular thing? Is God
asking her to let something go, inviting him to do less? If
time spent in prayer offers no clear direction, reason can
help. Here are some criteria for deciding, gleaned from St.
Ignatius: There is a clearly identifiable need. You have a
special gift or expertise others may not have. Others will
benefit. It's not contrary to church teaching or Scripture.

Philippians 3:3–8a
Psalm 105:2–3,4–5,6–7
Luke 15:1–10

What is this I hear about you?
Prepare a full account of your stewardship.
—LUKE 16:2

Preparing well for the sacrament of reconciliation doesn't
involve a mere review of the commandments. Some of us still
operate on definitions of sin designed for grade schoolers.
Have we been good stewards of familial relationships?
Turned our backs on God's love? When have we refused to
meet someone's need when it was in our power to address it?
Sin is a rupture in relationships. We even must consider the
relationship we hold with ourselves. Do we deny the
goodness God made in each of us? It's sinful to devalue
human dignity. As we take stock, think about what gifts were
ignored, misused, treated as entitlements, or assumed to be
the result of our own doing. God forgives extravagantly. The
way God loves sinners is confounding!

Philippians 3:17—4:1
Psalm 122:1–2,3–4ab,4cd–5
Luke 16:1–8

Saturday

NOVEMBER 5

> *It is not that I am eager for the gift;*
> *rather, I am eager for the profit that accrues*
> *to your account.*
> —PHILIPPIANS 4:17

Fundraisers know how important thank-you letters are. Paul,
who knew how to live simply, thanks the Philippians whose
generosity pleases God. Paul recalls how the readers sent him
money in Thessalonica. It feels great to be thanked. As Paul
speaks about having enough resources, he offers this hope:
"My God will fully [yes, fully] supply whatever you need
[not want], in accord with his glorious riches in Christ Jesus."
Are we grateful for resources we have? Today's readings are
all about wealth. Even the alleluia verse says that "Jesus
became poor although he was rich." Pharisees sneer at Jesus,
who admonishes them for coveting wealth and reputation.
Genuine riches consist of graces bestowed by the Holy
Spirit. One of these graces is gratitude.

Philippians 4:10–19
Psalm 112:1b–2,5–6,8a and 9
Luke 16:9–15

NOVEMBER 6

• THIRTY-SECOND SUNDAY IN ORDINARY TIME •

> [Jesus said,] "That the dead will rise
> even Moses made known in the passage about the bush
> when he called out 'Lord,'
> the God of Abraham, the God of Isaac, and the God of Jacob;
> and he is not God of the dead, but of the living,
> for to him all are alive."
> —LUKE 20:37–38

Material concerns can drive thoughts of the hereafter far away. "Is that all there is?" we ask the day after a perfect holiday or sumptuous meal. Fleeting mortal moments leave us unsatisfied and wanting more. We are very much mistaken if we think the best possible earthly *anything* can compare with life in God. Jesus promised resurrection and a future full of joy. No denying it. Might we visit with Moses in heaven, hear his experiences of the burning bush, or talk to Abraham about his willingness to risk Isaac in order to obey God?

2 Maccabees 7:1–2,9–14
Psalm 17:1,5–6,8,15 (15b)
2 Thessalonians 2:16—3:5
Luke 20:27–38

NOVEMBER 7

[Jesus said,] 'And if [your brother] wrongs you seven times in one day,
and returns to you seven times saying, 'I'm sorry,'
you should forgive him."
—LUKE 17:4

Jesus wisely warned the apostles to be on the watch for ways
that people inadvertently and inevitably collude with sin.
Woeful consequences will occur. Yet we humans stubbornly
have trouble forgiving others. We feel indignant: "Forgive
him? Really, Jesus? Why? People aren't supposed to be
doormats. He's the one who was wrong." Simultaneously, we
give ourselves a pass, refuse to notice where we neglected to
do good, and blame others if given an opportunity. A simple
sin can grow into a habit taken for granted. Soon that sin is
part of a structure in society: "Everybody's doing it." Jesus
invites us to point out sins for one another, and to forgive.

Titus 1:1–9
Psalm 24:1b–2,3–4ab,5–6
Luke 17:1–6

NOVEMBER 8

We await the blessed hope,
the appearance of the glory of the great God
and of our savior Jesus Christ,
who gave himself for us to deliver us
from all lawlessness
and to cleanse for himself a people as his own,
eager to do what is good.
—TITUS 2:13–14

After the Our Father at Mass, the priest's prayer includes "as we await the blessed hope." His words echo Paul's encouragement to Titus that becoming free from disordered desires is possible only due to God's saving grace. When the assembly at Mass prays to be delivered from evil, we are also asking to be kept from subtle evils like inordinate attachments. The prayer is a clear invitation to look ahead to the promise of heaven and to Jesus, who is our joyful hope. Enduring trials is easier when we focus on the goal: something far beyond this transitory life.

Titus 2:1–8,11–14
Psalm 37:3–4,18 and 23,27 and 29
Luke 17:7–10

NOVEMBER 9

• THE DEDICATION OF THE LATERAN BASILICA •

*Do you not know that you are the temple of God,
and that the Spirit of God dwells in you?*
—1 CORINTHIANS 3:16

Each of us is a walking basilica. Within these walls, a peaceful home is available. The soul kneels within, constantly worshiping the One who created the edifice of the human body. Treasured inside, the Holy Spirit dwells. Here is a space where one can let go of the burdens of one's own making and thus become free to shoulder the burdens of Christian loving.

Many people have experienced a friend saying, "I'll never forget when you said, . . ." yet the listener has no memory of saying it. God worked through the "building" of a welcoming heart, even when the person lacked awareness of it. May we keep our doors unlocked and available to visitors throughout the day.

Ezekiel 47:1–2,8–9,12
Psalm 46:2–3,5–6,8–9
1 Corinthians 3:9c–11,16–17
John 2:13–22

Jesus said in reply,
"The coming of the Kingdom of God
cannot be observed,
and no one will announce, 'Look, here it is,' or,
'There it is.'
For behold, the Kingdom of God is among you."
—LUKE 17:20B–21

Leo's Gift, published by Loyola Press, is a book for every age, about a boy who dares to act on the Holy Spirit's promptings after noticing a woman struggling to remember. Using music, he reawakens memory and elicits joy. The fictional character shares the name of a doctor of the church who knew Scripture well and preached in ways that touched everyday needs. The reign of God is among us when we listen attentively, connect with God, and act kindly to others. When God rules in our hearts, the kingdom has come.

Philemon 7–20
Psalm 146:7,8–9a,9bc–10
Luke 17:20–25

With all my heart I seek you.
—PSALM 119:10A

Everything on earth is here to help you reach the purpose for which you were created: to praise, reverence, and serve God, and as a result, find yourself in heaven someday. This paraphrase of a portion of St. Ignatius's Principle and Foundation suggests using things only if they lead to a closer relationship with the Almighty. Trying to live by this ideal is difficult to accomplish half-heartedly. Name something you pursue wholeheartedly. Compare it with the way you seek God. Are you "all in" or holding back? God wants you to seek. You *will* find. It may feel as if it all depends on your action, but God is drawing you, initiating contact, wooing you, and wanting your heart. You may choose a circuitous path, but even the act of seeking God is a grace you can request.

2 John 4–9
Psalm 119:1,2,10,11,17,18
Luke 17:26–37

NOVEMBER 12

• ST. JOSAPHAT, BISHOP AND MARTYR •

Jesus told his disciples a parable
about the necessity for them to pray always without
becoming weary.
—LUKE 18:1

I get tired of asking God for the same thing, whether it be release for me from a bad habit or the gift of a spouse for a friend who longs to be married. Today's parable suggests that God wants to be nagged! God, for some reason, likes to hear repeated requests. Is it because I will treasure the answer when it is finally given? A cold drink is even better when I'm so thirsty that my throat feels like the Sahara. Perhaps bothering God and persisting will result in greater gratitude on my part. I wonder if an increase in gratitude is the grace I need today. Or is it something else?

3 John 5–8
Psalm 112:1–2,3–4,5–6
Luke 18:1–8

Sunday

NOVEMBER 13

• THIRTY-THIRD SUNDAY IN ORDINARY TIME •

> *But for you who fear my name, there will arise*
> *the sun of justice with its healing rays.*
> —MALACHI 3:20A

Don't you feel special, singled out, as you read this clip from Malachi? Perhaps you hear the implication: *Just for you.* The healing rays you need will arrive—because you hold the name of the Most High God in awe. Think about an experience when knowing someone's name opened a door for you that would otherwise have remained shut. "Little girl, you can't come in here," the firefighter said. "But my last name is the same as your captain's. I'm his daughter," she replied. Immediately she was admitted. At a bank, the name signed on a check opened coffers of cash. Names matter. When it comes to God's name, doors of healing and grace fly open.

Malachi 3:19–20a
Psalm 98:5–6,7–8,9
2 Thessalonians 3:7–12
Luke 21:5–19

⮞ 351 ⮜

NOVEMBER 14

[Jesus asked,] "What do you want me to do for you?"
—LUKE 18:41

For whatever reasons, God wants us to name our desires and then ask for what we want. Jesus never forces his will upon us, but he invites us to say clearly what we want. We may not get it, because God knows what's best. Still, each and every day, we're invited to stop and think about what graces, or gifts, we will need today. Will it be courage to withstand physical suffering? Or patience to endure a mental trial? We may need generosity to get through a thousand requests for our time. As the liturgical year winds down, what graces will we need for the end of 2022? For the moment, let's identify and request the graces we need today.

Revelation 1:1–4; 2:1–5
Psalm 1:1–2,3,4 and 6
Luke 18:35–43

He who walks blamelessly and does justice;
who thinks the truth in his heart
—PSALM 15:2

The psalmist writes about the kind of people who walk with God and who will one day live in heaven. Mary walked to visit Elizabeth. Healed lepers walked back to show themselves to the priests. Jesus walked everywhere. Where will *your* footsteps take you today? Slow down and notice the way you walk. Your gait might reveal a person of joy, someone habitually rushing, or an oblivious soul thinking of the past or future but completely unaware of the present. Notice the steps of people around you. They could be burdened, self-absorbed, arrogant, or . . . something else. God wants lots of company in heaven. A community locks arms and uplifts the weak ones as we walk to our holy destination.

Revelation 3:1–6,14–22
Psalm 15:2–3a,3bc–4ab,5
Luke 19:1–10

NOVEMBER 16

Worthy are you, Lord our God,
to receive glory and honor and power,
for you created all things;
because of your will they came to be
and were created.
—REVELATION 4:11

I put the key in the door, and it sparked. Energy became visible in sheer radiance. I brushed someone's hand, and static electricity shocked us. So many created things are unseen, from distant galaxies to human emotions. The power of God is so unfathomable compared to my meager five senses, my intuitions, feelings, and reasoning. How can I possibly grasp the reality of God, who simply wills something and it comes into being? Yet God wants to be approachable and makes it possible through Jesus.

Revelation 4:1–11,
Psalm 150:1b–2,3–4,5–6
Luke 19:11–28

NOVEMBER 17

• ST. ELIZABETH OF HUNGARY, RELIGIOUS •

[Jesus] saw the city and wept over it, saying,
"If this day you only knew what makes for peace—
but now it is hidden from your eyes."
—LUKE 19:41–42

Jesus' sorrow showed deep human feeling as he stood near Jerusalem. Tears filled his eyes and spilled down his cheeks. He had such high hopes for this beautiful city on a hill, but it wouldn't be. How sad Jesus must have felt knowing that so many people, and especially his beloved Jewish community, would not recognize the Most High in their midst. Jesus had a hard life, full of temptations to give in to power grabs or to despair at the puny observable results of his work. He cried. Deep sadness is part of human experience. Hopes and dreams for peace are too.

Revelation 5:1–10
Psalm 149:1b–2,3–4,5–6a and 9b
Luke 19:41–44

• THE DEDICATION OF THE BASILICAS OF ST. PETER AND ST. PAUL, APOSTLES
* ST. ROSE PHILIPPINE DUCHESNE, VIRGIN •

They could find no way to accomplish
their purpose
because all the people were hanging on his words.
—LUKE 19:48

The Jewish leaders couldn't arrest Jesus because people were
mesmerized by the Good News. When was the last time you
were so enthralled by words that time flew? Think of a
speech that was so charismatic that you sat at the edge of
your seat, unconcerned about the time. Now see yourself in
the imposing temple in Jerusalem, where Jesus tells story
after story. You want him to talk on forever. *How will that one
about the tenant farmers end?* you wonder. Holding on to the
words of Jesus is a sure way to stave off evil, which cannot
accomplish its purpose while the community crowds around.
Cling to Jesus.

Revelation 10:8–11 or Acts 28:11–16,30–31
Psalm 119:14,24,72,103,111,131 or 98:1,2–3ab,3cd–4,5–6
Luke 19:45–48 or Matthew 14:22–33

NOVEMBER 19

*My mercy and my fortress,
my stronghold, my deliverer.*
—PSALM 144:2

Culture offers many false sanctuaries from better lives. Distractions such as games on phones, social media, and television lure people from doing something greater, such as taking time for prayer. When life wearies us, investing a few extra minutes in prayer can draw people into a strong, safe shelter. Storm clouds will pass, and it's more comfortable to wait them out with the Almighty. God stands ready with open arms to rescue the one running from fear, anxiety, stress, and temptation. When life is overwhelming, God offers strength and comfort. God is really the one in control. What diversions or avoidance behaviors sidetrack us from running to God as a hideout, a place to find respite, healing, and new energy to face it all?

Revelation 11:4–12
Psalm 144:1b,2,9–10
Luke 20:27–40

NOVEMBER 20

• OUR LORD JESUS CHRIST, KING OF THE UNIVERSE •

He is the image of the invisible God.
—COLOSSIANS 1:15

Years ago, in an IMAX theater, I witnessed a demo of the infrastructure, which became visible only when lights illuminated the space behind the screen. I felt terrified. The thin eight-story filmy surface disappeared, and ominous dark scaffolding took its place. I had no idea about the theater's massive integral structure. I was relieved when the lights in the theater came back on. Jesus, like the screen in front of the theater's skeleton, makes the omnipotent, omniscient One so much easier to approach. We know what God looks like: he looks like Jesus. Allow yourself time to sink into this truth and ponder it. You, too, are an image of the invisible God.

2 Samuel 5:1–3
Psalm 122:1–2,3–4,4–5
Colossians 1:12–20
Luke 23:35–43

NOVEMBER 21

• THE PRESENTATION OF THE BLESSED VIRGIN MARY •

See, I am coming to dwell among you, says the LORD.
—ZECHARIAH 2:14

As we consider Mary being brought in a traditional ceremony to be presented in the temple, we already know her future. God will be coming to dwell with humanity through her very flesh. Her body will be the temple. The food she eats will be transformed biologically through a complex process, and a completely separate human being will result. She will nurture Christ without even knowing how her uterus works. Six centuries before Mary's birth, Emmanuel was prophesied. Everyone believed he was coming. And here Mary is, a child in the temple, soon to become a sanctuary herself. Jesus is incarnate in us, too. When we receive Eucharist, our cells welcome his. Our flesh is the dwelling place of the Ancient of Days.

MEMORIAL
Zechariah 2:14–17
Luke 1:46–47,48–49,50–51,52–53,54–55
Matthew 12:46–50

Tuesday

NOVEMBER 22

• ST. CECILIA, VIRGIN AND MARTYR •

Let the heavens be glad and the earth rejoice;
let the sea and what fills it resound.
—PSALM 96:11

Bob Dufford, SJ, used this psalm to create an upbeat worship tune with the lyrics, "Let all creation sing!" Imagine walking outside right now and hearing every tree branch uplifted in audible praise. What might it sound like? Perhaps you've heard wind rustling leaves, or waves crashing on shore, or birdsong, and that made it easy to imagine creation making music.

The Feast of St. Cecilia, patron of music, is a great day to spend some time appreciating melodies. Music as prayer connects beyond the mind into a gut-level response. Even if God gave you a voice like a croaking frog, dare to sing loudly with all of creation and praise God, who loves to hear the voices created for this purpose.

Revelation 14:14–19
Psalm 96:10,11–12,13
Luke 21:5–11

NOVEMBER 23

• ST. CLEMENT I, POPE AND MARTYR • ST. COLUMBAN, ABBOT • BLESSED
MIGUEL AUGUSTÍN PRO, PRIEST AND MARTYR •

*[Jesus said,] "They will seize and persecute you;
they will hand you over to the synagogues and
to prisons,
and they will have you led before kings and governors
because of my name."*
—LUKE 21:12B

Viva, Cristo Rey! shouted Blessed Miguel Pro as he died before
a firing squad in 1927. "Long live Christ the King!" The
Mexican priest donned many disguises, from beggar to
businessman, policeman to old woman, to evade capture and
carry out his clandestine pastoral ministry. The church
endured many persecutions in the early decades of the last
century, and many Mexicans died for their faith. The jovial
priest risked everything, regardless of his government's
policy, and was assassinated at age thirty-six. Today calls
forth memories of last Sunday's feast. "Viva, Cristo Rey!"

Revelation 15:1–4
Psalm 98:1,2–3ab,7–8,9
Luke 21:12–19

NOVEMBER 24

• ST. ANDREW DŨNG-LAC, PRIEST, AND COMPANIONS, MARTYRS •
THANKSGIVING DAY •

I give thanks to my God always on your account.
—1 CORINTHIANS 1:4

Our weekly women's group learned from our regular waitress
that every employee in the restaurant is required to work at
least four hours on both Thanksgiving and Christmas. It made
me wonder about all the people making my life better while I
know little if anything about what they experience, and even
suffer. Cashiers, cooks, busboys, and gardeners came to mind.
Our group decided that in addition to our usual tips we would
each write our waitress a thank-you note for her service all year
long. Is there someone you can thank today?

Revelation 18:1–2,21–23; 19:1–3,9a	**PROPER MASS IN THANKSGIVING**
Psalm 100:1b–2,3,4,5	**TO GOD:**
Luke 21:20–28	Sirach 50:22–24
	1 Corinthians 1:3–9
	Luke 17:11–19

Friday

NOVEMBER 25

• ST. CATHERINE OF ALEXANDRIA, VIRGIN AND MARTYR •

[Jesus said,] "Consider the fig tree and all the other trees.
When their buds burst open,
you see for yourselves and know that summer
is now near."
—LUKE 21:29B–30

Jesus saw beauty. It gave him an idea for a lesson he wanted
to teach. Perhaps he was puzzling over the best way to
describe the need to pay attention to the signs of God's reign
bursting forth. Maybe the thought came to him in a rush.
Were the disciples looking downward, complaining about
sore feet, or eyeballing each other with jealousy? Walking
with Jesus, the followers may have been seeing without
seeing. Or maybe Jesus noticed James and Andrew staring up
at the tree branches, jaws slack. Jesus made connections
between his physical environment and the spiritual realm.
"Look at the signs!" Jesus might have said. "Signposts of love
are all around."

Revelation 20:1–4,11—21:2
Psalm 84:3,4,5–6a and 8a
Luke 21:29–33

NOVEMBER 26

The LORD is a great God,
and a great king above all gods;
In his hands are the depths of the earth,
and the tops of the mountains are his.
—PSALM 95:3–4

During a mission trip, Sister Lalli introduced her roommate to the breviary, a prayer form that includes Psalm 95 every morning. The psalmist instills awe while calling the reader to praise God. "Sister, I can picture a transcendent God who cups the oceans in a loving hand, enjoys scooping up a family of whales, and returns them to the sea before they've even noticed God was at work," said the woman new to the breviary. "God gives Mount Everest a little pat on its peak with a majestic touch and blows kisses of snowfall." Sister Lalli smiled. She had her own favorite images to describe God's power in creation. What are yours?

Revelation 22:1–7
Psalm 95:1–2,3–5,6–7ab
Luke 21:34–36

NOVEMBER 27

• FIRST SUNDAY OF ADVENT •

[Jesus said,] "Two men will be out in the field;
one will be taken, and one will be left."
—MATTHEW 24:40

Several people died this week: a twentysomething girl, a
woman in her late fifties, a ninety-plus relative, and some
parishioners. Why does one person leave for heaven and
another is still here? "Why am *I* here?" asks an octogenarian
whom I call weekly. "So we can have this conversation!" I tease.
I have no good answer for her. Is there some service she has yet
to do? I don't know. Jesus may return for her or me today. A
new liturgical year offers the opportunity to consider what I
might do today to be ready for whenever God comes. If I live
today with appreciation, it may be easier to ask for the grace of
indifference about when my last day will be.

Isaiah 2:1–5
Psalm 122:1–2,3–4,4–5,6–7,8–9
Romans 13:11–14
Matthew 24:37–44

NOVEMBER 28

"Peace be within you!"
—PSALM 122:8

Daily meditation is a good habit to consider for Advent. Try
this. See in your mind's eye a stack of blank paper. Sit
comfortably and "look" at the paper. Ask God to be present;
wait for God to manifest. Keep your eyes closed as you focus
on the blank page. Maybe it'll be Christ's face that appears.
Or a fuzzy image or word. Don't force anything. It's more
likely that distractions will appear (I forgot my vitamins. . . .).
When that happens, mentally move that sheet off to the side
or even push it to the floor. You can address that distraction
later. Look at the fresh blank page. Soon you may notice that
your breathing has slowed or become rhythmic. Let that go
also. Wait expectantly for God. Sometimes repeating a word
or two helps you focus. "I'm here." Be patient.

Isaiah 4:2–6
Psalm 122:1–2,3–4b,4cd–5,6–7,8–9
Matthew 8:5–11

NOVEMBER 29

[Jesus said,] "I give you praise, Father, Lord of heaven and earth."
—LUKE 10:21

Advent's watchword is *waiting*. Prayer can be thought of as spending time expectantly waiting for God. Often we do the opposite. We come to prayer with lists of requests and things we want to tell God. Building on yesterday's reflection, let's ask ourselves if we're willing to wait for God to lead prayer today. A repeated word or words of praise can set the tone: "I praise you." Jesus models this in today's Gospel. We were created to praise, reverence, and serve God. It might help remove the distraction of time by setting a timer before we even begin. Whether to choose five, twenty, or forty-five minutes to start depends on our existing prayer habits. Revisit the blank paper from yesterday when distractions surface. Some of us will need to visualize large poster boards to quiet our distractions.

Isaiah 11:1–10
Psalm 72:1–2,7–8,12–13,17
Luke 10:21–24

$\mathcal{W}ednesday$

NOVEMBER 30

• ST. ANDREW, APOSTLE •

He called them, and immediately
they left their boat and their father
and followed him.
—MATTHEW 4:21–22

Let's say you wake up late but move to your favorite prayer
chair anyway. You want to listen for God, but the phone
rings. You respond to the caller and return to the psalm of
the day. Then a ping interrupts. It's a text from a friend who
needs prayer *now*. Is this God calling or a distraction? How
will you choose? Do you stay with formal prayer or leave
"your boat" to follow Jesus in service? God's calls are
mysterious, and it takes practice to sort out the day's
messages. God continually beckons, and we respond,
sometimes with small acts of love. Some people hide their
phones while they pray; others keep them handy. It's up to
you to discern how best to listen for God.

Romans 10:9–18
Psalm 19:8,9,10,11
Matthew 4:18–22

DECEMBER 1

*[Jesus said,] "Everyone who listens to these words of mine and acts
on them
will be like a wise man who built his house on rock."*
—MATTHEW 7:24

"It's too hard. I can't keep up this pace. Maybe I should give up."
When tempted to skip Advent praying, double down. Maybe
the blank-paper meditation isn't working for you. Try a
different prayer practice, like Scripture reading. We all have
our own native praying places. For some, it's listening to music.
For others, it's putting ourselves into the Gospel scene.
Whatever you try, stay with the amount of prayer time you
promised yourself when Advent began. Some days will be
harder than others. That's okay. You may even forget on a
couple of days. That doesn't give you a pass to quit. Start fresh.
Each day is a new beginning. Prayer is your firm foundation.

Isaiah 26:1–6
Psalm 118:1 and 8–9,19–21,25–27a
Matthew 7:21,24–27

*Jesus warned them sternly,
"See that no one knows about this."
But they went out and spread the word of him through all
that land.*
—MATTHEW 9:30–31

The minute Jesus grants a spectacular gift, people turn
around and completely disobey a stern command. What
motivated their complete disregard for Jesus' wishes? It could
have been joy. Imagine you've just been cured of blindness.
"I'm only telling you, and one other person," you say as
justification for spreading the word. A chain reaction results,
and quickly the secret is widely known. The minute Jesus
grants me forgiveness, I turn around and repeat a mistake.
I've no excuse. It's a shameful and confusing condition. We
are all loved sinners, and there is no violation that God
cannot forgive. Thank God that God is all merciful.

Isaiah 29:17–24
Psalm 27:1,4,13–14
Matthew 9:27–31

From behind, a voice shall sound in your ears:
"This is the way; walk in it,"
when you would turn to the right or to the left.
—ISAIAH 30:21

Parents often get credit for having eyes in the back of their heads. They know to investigate when things get too quiet, or to check out that mischievous giggle. Parents are paying attention. So must we. God is whispering all the time, and what a consoling thought this is! A man gets "a funny feeling" and exits the freeway one stop early, only to find a neighbor in great distress over a car problem at the intersection. An unexplainable hint moves someone to send a text just when a friend desperately needs encouragement. A voice is sounding. Following it will allow God to make straight our path despite our crooked and feeble performances.

Isaiah 30:19–21,23–26
Psalm 147:1–2,3–4,5–6
Matthew 9:35—10:1,5a,6–8

Sunday

DECEMBER 4

• SECOND SUNDAY OF ADVENT •

Then the wolf will be a guest of the lamb.
—ISAIAH 11:6

It's one of the shocking truths of our faith: God wants
eagerly, almost wantonly, to forgive even the bloodthirsty
among us. Picture Christ as a fluffy and vulnerable lamb,
setting the table with the finest meal—one beyond compare.
You are one of the invited guests. The doorbell rings, and in
strolls a hairy, smelly wolf. He's brought a bottle of wine, and
he gives the lamb a hug. It's risky to invite a wolf into one's
home and easy to jump to judgment or recoil in fear. Daring
to love sinners is risky. Yet Christ never gives up inviting
people. The reign of God among us means that we need to
keep inviting also. Jesus models behavior that disciples are
challenged to follow.

Isaiah 11:1–10
Psalm 72:1–2,7–8,12–13,17
Romans 15:4–9
Matthew 3:1–12

DECEMBER 5

Pharisees and teachers of the law,
who had come from every village of Galilee and
Judea and Jerusalem,
were sitting there, and the power of the Lord was with [Jesus] for healing.
—LUKE 5:17

I wonder if Jesus looked at these leaders and remembered being twelve years old, when his parents found him in the temple. "Here I am again," I can hear him thinking to himself. "I astounded some of these very old men back then. I wonder if they recognize me. How much I've grown, and learned. They were astounded then. They will be astonished again as I continue about my father's business." A slow smile creeps across Jesus' gentle face as he sees the eyes of a teacher looking at him with longing. Jesus recognizes the wordless request, nods, and looks him straight in the eye. Without a word, Jesus heals the man's hidden addiction.

Isaiah 35:1–10
Psalm 85:9ab and 10,11–12,13–14
Luke 5:17–26

DECEMBER 6

• ST. NICHOLAS, BISHOP •

Jesus said to his disciples:
"What is your opinion?"
—MATTHEW 18:12

This isn't the only time Scripture records Jesus soliciting
feedback from the audience. Sometimes he questions his
enemies. Jesus constantly challenged people to examine their
points of view. Jesus was—and is—genuinely interested in
what people think. And he knows that people often learn by
hearing themselves say something out loud. This is one
reason people see counselors and therapists. Jesus understood
that moving around to where a person stands right now is the
best place to connect and to begin a conversation. It's like
two blind people arguing about what an elephant is while
one holds the tail and the other the ear. When people "walk
around the elephant" to hear another's perspective, common
ground and better understanding are more easily established.
Start with the other's opinion before eagerly giving
your own.

Isaiah 40:1–11
Psalm 96:1–2,3 and 10ac,11–12,13
Matthew 18:12–14

Merciful and gracious is the LORD,
slow to anger and abounding in kindness.
Not according to our sins does he deal with us,
nor does he requite us according to our crimes.
—PSALM 103:8,10

Generation after generation has trouble believing the good news of God's outrageous love. The psalmist knew how God brims with kindness. It's shocking really, to consider how God is more eager to dole out mercy than punishment. A psalm like this is a consoling prescription for a soul discouraged and spiraling into negative feelings. Rather than give up because of personal failures, the soul who focuses on how great God is will find the courage and energy to weather the latest difficulties. God never gives up on the beloved.

Isaiah 40:25–31
Psalm 103:1–2,3–4,8 and 10
Matthew 11:28–30

• THE IMMACULATE CONCEPTION OF THE BLESSED VIRGIN MARY (PATRONAL
FEAST DAY OF THE UNITED STATES OF AMERICA) •

All the ends of the earth have seen
the salvation by our God.
—PSALM 98:3D

When I first memorized the words of the *Memorare* in first grade, I had no idea what it meant. Now it's a favorite because it relies on the sure knowledge that salvation has come through Mary into the person of Jesus. To paraphrase, "Remember, Mary, that everyone who comes to you for help gets it. This inspires me to run to you today, Mom, sorrowful sinner that I am. I trust you to take my requests to your obedient Son, who loves making you happy. I know you won't laugh at my petitions, but you'll go ahead and present them to the God of Mercy. Thanks!" Using the intercession of others builds my confidence.

Genesis 3:9–15,20
Psalm 98:1,2–3ab,3cd–4
Ephesians 1:3–6,11–12
Luke 1:26–38

Friday
DECEMBER 9
• ST. JUAN DIEGO CUAUHTLATOATZIN, HERMIT •

I, the LORD, your God,
teach you what is for your good,
and lead you on the way you should go.
—ISAIAH 48:17

We have no idea what God is capable of doing, and we haven't even conceived of what God can do in our lives. We benefit from always looking to Jesus to learn which way to go. Jesus lived an apparently small, ordinary life for thirty years. He demonstrated that mundane, run-of-the-mill days have meaning. Who in his backwater town would have thought that Jesus' words would echo around the globe for centuries! Never underestimate the power of God to do something majestic through our small and seemingly insignificant actions. God loves working this way.

Isaiah 48:17–19
Psalm 1:1–2,3,4 and 6
Matthew 11:16–19

DECEMBER 10

• OUR LADY OF LORETO •

Blessed is he who shall have seen you
and who falls asleep in your friendship.
—SIRACH 48:11

In Loreto, Italy, is a house said to be the home of Mary, brought there by a family by the surname of Angelo, giving rise to stories that the Nazorean abode was carried there by angels. Imagine the hospitality you might find in Mary's home and how comfortable you might feel spending a quiet evening there with Jesus. Perhaps there's a fire burning, and Mary is mending. Imagine that Jesus is telling you a story, maybe one of your favorite parables. Imagine feeling so at ease that you doze off as his comforting voice gently calms your weary heart. Don't fret about anything. Let yourself rest in the friendship of this gentle son and mother. How can we make our homes welcoming spaces for Jesus in return?

Sirach 48:1–4,9–11
Psalm 80:2ac and 3b,15–16,18–19
Matthew 17:9a,10–13

DECEMBER 11

• THIRD SUNDAY OF ADVENT •

See how the farmer waits for the precious fruit
of the earth,
being patient with it
until it receives the early and the late rains.
You too must be patient.
—JAMES 5:7B–8A

Eating seasonally is good for the earth, uses fewer resources, and allows us to appreciate foods in due season. But it means a long wait until apricots or strawberries are in season again. Food can be frozen, dried, canned, cooked, preserved, or grown in hot-houses. No such control with God's action. Faith involves a great deal of patience as we wait for prayers to be answered, for graces to be granted, and for Christ's second coming. God cannot be forced to appear on demand. When making a decision to wait on the Lord, keep in mind that it may take a long time. Pray and wait.

Isaiah 35:1–6a,10
Psalm 146:6–7,8–9,9–10
James 5:7–10
Matthew 11:2–11

Monday
DECEMBER 12
• OUR LADY OF GUADALUPE •

Silence, all [people], in the presence of the LORD! For he stirs forth from his holy dwelling.
—ZECHARIAH 2:17

About five hundred years before Jesus was conceived in the womb of Our Lady, the prophet Zechariah spoke of God living with humanity. In that context, waiting for Christ seems the epitome of patience. The hearers of the prophecy were invited to rejoice in the future event, to experience joy in their current reality. It was a call to expectant hope. Waiting would be rewarded. They counted on it. Fast forward to today. God dwells with humanity here and now. Look around! Faith will reveal God-with-us, Emmanuel, in the people we meet today. And the same forward-focused hope surrounds our present, waiting for the invitation to dwell with God in heaven forever.

Zechariah 2:14–17 or Revelation 11:19a; 12:1–6a,10ab
Judith 13:18bcde,19
Luke 1:26–38 or 1:39–47

DECEMBER 13

• ST. LUCY, VIRGIN AND MARTYR •

The LORD is close to the brokenhearted.
—PSALM 34:19

A parent's heart goes out to the child who just fell off a bike and is crying pitifully. Running to the child's side, the parent wraps the wounded one in loving arms. The other children, safe in the house, go about their homework and chores, trusting that if their hearts break, that parent will be there for them as well. Zephaniah cites trust as an important foundation for a blessed life. People who take refuge in humble trust can relax into the protection of Abba, Jesus' term for God the Father. God runs to the beloved whenever spirits are crushed.

Zephaniah 3:1–2,9–13
Psalm 34:2–3,6–7,17–18,19 and 23
Matthew 21:28–32

DECEMBER 14

• ST. JOHN OF THE CROSS, PRIEST AND DOCTOR OF THE CHURCH •

[Jesus said,] "Go and tell John what you have seen and heard:
the blind regain their sight,
the lame walk,
lepers are cleansed,
the deaf hear."
—LUKE 7:22

My doctor asked if I experienced additional ringing in my ears when I felt vertigo. "I don't know," I replied. He asked if I noticed a change in hearing during an episode. "I don't know," I said. He asked if I felt additional pressure in the air when it happened. "I don't know." How foolish I felt! What I *did* realize was that I hadn't been paying attention at all. I decided to redouble my efforts at noticing my hearing. It involved a conscious choice, a couple of alarms on my smartphone, and self-discipline. Our spiritual life requires a similar single-hearted approach to God's subtle communications with us.

Isaiah 45:6c–8,18,21c–25
Psalm 85:9ab and 10,11–12,13–14
Luke 7:18b–23

DECEMBER 15

Raise a glad cry, you barren one who did not bear,
break forth in jubilant song, you who were not in labor.
—ISAIAH 54:1

When's the last time you broke out singing? In a way that expressed deep joy and enthusiasm? When have you let out a whoop of joy so loud that someone looked at you funny? It's not something you see every day. People are more restrained as a rule. What was the news that caused you to erupt in an extraordinary way? Some celebratory sounds are saved for big things, like news of a pregnancy long desired. The prophet's reason for inviting you to this unrestrained exaltation is God's tender love, which will never leave you, and an endless mercy offered in an unbreakable covenant of peace. Let yourself sing and shout in relief and euphoria!

Isaiah 54:1–10
Psalm 30:2 and 4,5–6,11–12a and 13b
Luke 7:24–30

DECEMBER 16

*[Jesus said,] "John was a burning and shining lamp,
and for a while you were content to rejoice
in his light.
But I have a testimony greater than John's"*
—JOHN 5:35–36

As long as John talked about a Messiah yet to come, the Jews
weren't concerned about the fanatic in the desert. After
defying convention by curing on the Sabbath, Jesus opens a
dialogue with people who are furious. They don't want this
kind of Messiah. After all these centuries of waiting, the
people don't expect a humble leader like Jesus. They argue
against miracles. Jesus stays and talks with passion, trying his
best to reason with them. After all, he was sent to the Jews
first. Jesus doesn't give up on his detractors. Perhaps some
will be converted by this exchange of words. Having a
conversation with those who disagree with us is a means of
following Christ.

Isaiah 56:1–3a,6–8
Psalm 67:2–3,5,7–8
John 5:33–36

DECEMBER 17

The scepter shall never depart from Judah.
—GENESIS 49:10

Enter the mind of Jacob for a moment. His life is ending, and he reflects on the marvelous miracles he has experienced, including wrestling with a being who renamed him Israel. He recalls conspiring to obtain primacy in the family, thanks to a conniving mother who kept Isaac from giving Esau the fatherly blessing. God was with him through it all, not providing for Jacob because of his worthiness, but because God willed it. And now he looks at twelve sons, and some divine insight alerts him that the fourth in line, Judah, will be top dog. These are the same brothers who sold the youngest into slavery out of jealousy. When they heard their dad make this prediction, how did the brothers take this news of a future ruler outside the usual succession?

Genesis 49:2,8–10
Psalm 72:1–2,3–4ab,7–8,17
Matthew 1:1–17

DECEMBER 18

• FOURTH SUNDAY OF ADVENT •

*Grace to you and peace from God our Father
and the Lord Jesus Christ.*
—ROMANS 1:7

Advent waiting is softened by knowing that soon loved ones
will be exchanging greetings and peaceful wishes. We will
make new memories, reenact traditions, and enjoy special
foods. For those who grieve their first holiday season after
the death of someone dear, waiting may be less peaceful. As
followers of Christ, we experience the mystery of the
Resurrection juxtaposed with lives touched by crucifixion.
Families in developing countries wait for rain to help them
eke out a meager harvest. Unemployed workers wait for a
call from a prospective employer, not knowing if their
financial cushion will last in what has already been months of
struggle. Those who wait indefinitely need our prayers today.
May they experience grace sufficient for their trials and
genuine peace in their struggles.

Isaiah 7:10–14
Psalm 24:1–2,3–4,5–6 (7c and 10b)
Romans 1:1–7
Matthew 1:18–24

DECEMBER 19

On you I depend from birth;
from my mother's womb you are my strength.
—PSALM 71:6

We usually take daily breath for granted. One flows after the
other. It's too easy to forget that we depend utterly on God
from our first breath on. As babies we have no need to worry
about anything. God provides and strengthens the
developing intellect, muscles, and soul. God loves to watch
us keep growing. At what point did God reveal to you that
all your growth was being supported by a divine force? In
what ways have you acknowledged that God is your strength
and that you depend utterly on God? Is there a concrete step
you can take to better acknowledge this?

Judges 13:2–7,24–25a
Psalm 71:3–4a,5–6ab,16–17
Luke 1:5–25

DECEMBER 20

*[The angel said,] "Do not be afraid, Mary,
for you have found favor with God."*
—LUKE 1:30

Have you ever substituted your name for Mary's in this verse?
God is pleased with us, too. We are beloved creations.
Flawed, but unique and precious. However, an angel
suddenly appearing in the room would certainly cause
anyone to leap out of their skin. It's not surprising, then, that
when God approaches us with a divine call, it might be
intimidating at first. It's natural to balk, or even resist. We
cannot rule out a vocation simply because it will be difficult.
In fact, recognizing that a call will involve self-sacrifice is
often a sign of God's genuine invitation. We need to consider
what it might cost to answer God's call. God's requests aren't
always easy, but we will experience a hopeful peace when we
are on the right track.

Isaiah 7:10–14
Psalm 24:1–2,3–4ab,5–6
Luke 1:26–38

He will sing joyfully because of you,
as one sings at festivals.
—ZEPHANIAH 3:17–18

Annual parish festivals build community. In one California city, people prepare for almost all year and draw visitors from far and wide. The junk booth, country store, international food booths, and midway games all take effort and pre-planning to pull off a fun-filled Friday-night-through-Sunday extravaganza. Carnival rides fill the front parking lot, and neighbors get free tickets to thank them for the noise they endure. Local musicians pull in crowds to the main stage. Dancing stops only at the neighborhood curfew. Children wish that the festival could occur every day. See in your imagination how God rejoices over you right now. Visualize an enormous party in your honor, waiting for you in heaven.

Song of Songs 2:8–14 or Zephaniah 3:14–18a
Psalm 33:2–3,11–12,20–21
Luke 1:39–45

DECEMBER 22

I prayed for this child, and the LORD granted my request.
Now I, in turn, give him to the LORD.
—1 SAMUEL 2:27–28A

Hannah's unwavering faith drove her to persistent, heartfelt prayer. What kind of discernment leads a mother to dedicate her firstborn son to God? Hannah had more children after Samuel, but she gave her first to temple service. Like Mary, Hannah offered her son to God as a type of Passover lamb.

All three readings today overflow with joy. Hannah's exuberant canticle prefigures Mary's. Returning Samuel to God was going to benefit others; it was outwardly good, and it was motivated by love. She gave out of gratitude. Leaving her son at the temple didn't mean that she never saw him again. Rather, she was detached enough to share her most precious son even though it must have been difficult. Freely received; freely given.

1 Samuel 1:24–28
1 Samuel 2:1,4–5,6–7,8abcd
Luke 1:46–56

"What, then, will this child be?
For surely the hand of the Lord was with him."
—LUKE 1:66

A Korean tradition called the *doljabi* attempts to reveal to
eager parents some information about their child's future.
Objects such as food, string, money, and books are placed on
a table. Parents watch the one-year-old choose. Will their
child never go hungry, live a long life, be wealthy, or become
a scholar? Zechariah may have wished for a son to follow
him into traditional priestly service. Not exactly what the
angel revealed. John wouldn't have a safe, quiet life or a long
one. John would be the prophetic voice, with the power of
Elijah, who would precede the Messiah. Poor Zechariah!
Perhaps disappointment struck Zechariah speechless. Did it
take him all the months of pregnancy to resign himself to a
different kind of son?

Malachi 3:1–4,23–24
Psalm 25:4–5ab,8–9,10 and 14
Luke 1:57–66

DECEMBER 24

In the tender compassion of our God
the dawn from on high shall break upon us.
—LUKE 1:78

When I was a child, Christmas began on the Eve. We opened gifts this night, after a family rosary. The focus was on the tender gift of God: Jesus. Sunday morning was strictly for Mass, with no need to rush home to open presents. To this day, during the Christmas Eve meal, we share *oplatky*, which is unleavened bread embossed with scenes of the Nativity. The oldest person is served first; a cross drawn in honey symbolizes the sweetness of our God. We retell how Jesus was laid in a place where animals ate. This hints at Jesus our Eucharist. On this holy night, we celebrate the body of Christ. Incarnation is a mind-blowing reality. What traditions mean most to you?

2 Samuel 7:1–5,8b–12,14a,16
Psalm 89:2–3,4–5,27 and 29
Luke 1:67–79

DECEMBER 25

• THE NATIVITY OF THE LORD (CHRISTMAS) •

Now this is how the birth of Jesus Christ came about.
—MATTHEW 1:18

"Joachim and I are also of David's house. So we, too, traveled to Bethlehem for the census. My poor daughter Mary had a tough time of it. Thank God I was with her at the stable when none of us could find accommodations. I'd presided at births before, but this one was special. I knew who the baby's father is. Mary dug her fingernails into my hand as she struggled to give life to her son. I bathed my perfectly formed grandson with a little water after Mary's difficult labor. Why did God allow my daughter to suffer so much? I did all I could to bring comfort to the new mother. In the future, an old man in the temple would predict more suffering for my Mary."

VIGIL:	DAWN:
Isaiah 62:1–5	Isaiah 62:11–12
Psalm 89:4–5,16–17,27,29 (2a)	Psalm 97:1,6,11–12
Acts 13:16–17,22–25	Titus 3:4–7
Matthew 1:1–25 or 1:18–25	Luke 2:15–20

NIGHT:	DAY:
Isaiah 9:1–6	Isaiah 52:7–10
Psalm 96:1–2,2–3,11–12,13	Psalm 98:1,2–3,3–4,5–6 (3c)
Titus 2:11–14	Hebrews 1:1–6
Luke 2:1–14	John 1:1–18 or 1:1–5, 9–14

Monday

DECEMBER 26

Stephen, filled with grace and power,
was working great wonders and signs
among the people.
—ACTS 6:8

Sufferings are very much a part of the Christmas story, from Mary traveling while nine months pregnant to her delivery in a stable. The birth of the early church also suffered difficulties, including the stoning of one of its first deacons. As the first martyr, Stephen gave his life because he spoke truthfully to very powerful leaders. The Holy Spirit makes such daring behavior possible. Somewhere in the world today, a modern-day Stephen is stepping out with courage to risk death by speaking against injustice. The Christmas narrative is not far from the Passion story; they are linked by love, determination, and fortitude. Will today offer us an opportunity to take some brave action in standing up for the love of Christ?

Acts 6:8–10; 7:54–59
Psalm 31:3cd–4,6 and 8ab,16bc and 17
Matthew 10:17–22

DECEMBER 27

• ST. JOHN, APOSTLE AND EVANGELIST •

What we have seen and heard
we proclaim now to you.
—1 JOHN 1:3A

John seems to be one of the more famous apostles, having been singled out on several occasions, including the Transfiguration, to accompany Jesus. Oh, the things John saw! If Jesus had chosen you to be an apostle, how would your life have impacted Jesus' ministry? Would you ask him to heal your family? Would people be jealous of you, or would Jesus be the kind of friend who never instilled envy in anyone? You might be tempted to brag about being one of the chosen Twelve. Would you say yes to taking care of Mary had you been asked at the cross, as John was? Imagine being Jesus' best friend. Think about your own close friends and what makes them so. Is Jesus in this category of friends?

1 John 1:1–4
Psalm 97:1–2,5–6,11–12
John 20:1a and 2–8

DECEMBER 28

• THE HOLY INNOCENTS, MARTYRS •

Joseph rose and took the child and his mother by night
and departed for Egypt.
—MATTHEW 2:14

Less than twenty-four hours old, she opened her eyes and looked at me. At me. I barely knew her mom, who had fled danger. As a volunteer at the United States–Mexico border, I served Christ who was disguised in the poor. I pondered, *Who did Jesus see on his first day of life?* I imagined Jesus looking at me now as I held this baby. I felt awe as she stared at one of the first human faces her eyes had seen. I leaned in. "You will see many wonders in this world," I whispered. I see wonders too. When she and I meet in heaven, I hope she'll recognize me as one of the first people she saw the day she was born.

1 John 1:5—2:2
Psalm 124:2–3,4–5,7cd–8
Matthew 2:13–18

DECEMBER 29

The darkness is passing away,
and the true light is already shining.
—1 JOHN 2:8B

The bright kitchen light diminished my small candle, which I
lit on the breakfast table to remind me I am not alone. I
placed the candle in the shadow of my coffee cup where it
shone brighter. I had a notion from somewhere deep within:
I think it was God. We need the shadows to help our light be
more evident. God uses my darkness—my sins—to make my
God-given light more evident. It's not me shining but the
Lord. I need not fear my shadows. It is there where Christ's
light shines even stronger. In darkness a light seems brighter.
God knows how to employ the darkness to help me and our
world shine a little brighter.

1 John 2:3–11
Psalm 96:1–2a,2b–3,5b–6
Luke 2:22–35

The angel of the Lord appeared in a dream to Joseph.
—MATTHEW 2:19

Joseph trusted his dreams more than once. In faith, he knew that God communicated to him through them, whether it meant he needed to marry Mary, flee Bethlehem, or return to Nazareth. God knew how Joseph listened best. Perhaps when Joseph attended synagogue, he felt distracted by his next carpentry commission and had trouble praying. Maybe his mind wandered during the reading of the Torah. God's conversation style is unique to each person. Some hear God best in song lyrics, others in apophatic silence. "I had this idea out of nowhere," someone might say. God uses different communication styles with different people. Dreams were Joseph's. Take some time to reflect on how you best listen to and hear God.

Sirach 3:2–6,12–14 or Colossians 3:12–21 or 3:12–17
Psalm 128:1–2,3,4–5
Matthew 2:13–15,19–23

• ST. THOMAS BECKET, BISHOP AND MARTYR •

Saturday

DECEMBER 31

• ST. SYLVESTER I, POPE •

In the beginning was the Word,
and the Word was with God,
and the Word was God.
—JOHN 1:1

A new calendar year begins tomorrow, but the liturgical year is
into its second season already. The Advent season is over; the
Christmas season wanes, too. Society pauses to look
backward; every Christian looks ahead with joyful hope. The
beginning of creation took place with Christ right there. Jesus
is the Word spoken. Do you feel the mystery? Let's endeavor
together to speak words of encouragement today,
participating in the Word which is with God and *is* God. The
Word was made flesh and now dwells within us. It's just too
marvelous to understand. May God's Word stay always deep
within each of us; may it be clearly heard and readily followed.
May we begin a new year with gratitude and joyful hope.

1 John 2:18–21
Psalm 96:1–2,11–12,13
John 1:1–18

ABOUT THE AUTHOR

Loretta Pehanich is an Ignatian-trained spiritual director with a lifetime in ministry and service, including 20 years in small faith-sharing groups. She leads retreats and workshops on prayer and busy lifestyles. Loretta is a founder of a women's ministry at St. Francis in Sacramento, California. Her other books are *Fleeting Moments: Praying When You Are Too Busy* and *Stand Up! Women in Conversation*. She and her husband, Steve, have 4 children and 10 grandchildren. Read her blogs at IgnatianSpirituality.com.

A VIBRANT PRAYER LIFE UNFOLDS when we regularly open ourselves to inspiration and God's grace. *2022: A Book of Grace-Filled Days* provides a daily prayer experience to help us build and nurture our faith.

Beginning with the start of the church year in Advent 2021 and continuing through the 2022 calendar year, this daily devotional notes major feast days, saint commemorations, and holidays. Each page combines readings from the Scripture of the day with reflections to offer a few minutes of solace for quiet prayer and meditation. *2022: A Book of Grace-Filled Days* is an accessible and insightful way to deepen our connection to God's loving presence and fill each day with grace.

LORETTA PEHANICH is an Ignatian-trained spiritual director with a lifetime in ministry and service, including 20 years in small faith-sharing groups. She leads retreats and workshops on prayer and busy lifesty[...] [...]en's ministry at St. Francis Pari[...] [...]her books are *Fleeting Moments: P[...]* [...]*Stand Up! Women in Conversation*. She and her husband, Steve, have 4 children and 10 grandchildren. Read her blogs at IgnatianSpirituality.com.

LOYOLAPRESS.
A JESUIT MINISTRY

www.loyolapress.com
Chicago

ISBN: 978-0-8294-5041-5

9 780829 450415